First published 2014
©Maureen Cubitt

ISBN 978–1–907750-88-5

The Author can be contacted via
www.mancroftbells.co.uk

Printed by Swallowtail Print Ltd
Unit 2, Drayton Industrial Park, Drayton, Norwich NR8 6RL
Telephone: 01603 868862

ACKNOWLEDGEMENTS

I should like to thank my husband David for his years of research into the history of Mancroft bells, his editing, proof reading and knowledgeable support in the preparation of this book.

Thanks also to staff at the Norfolk Record Office and the Norfolk Millennium Library, to Norfolk County Council and the Eastern Daily Press for the use of photographs. My thanks to John Eisel for information obtained from his volumes of newspaper extracts on ringing and to Tom Roast, for his work on 19th century Norfolk newspapers. I am grateful to Neil Thomas who photographed the ringers' artifacts and peal boards and to Richard Carter, who thought of the title. My thanks to Trish and Eric Hitchins and David Cubitt for their financial support and to Simon Smith for the final proof reading. Last, but by no means least, I owe gratitude for the support of the members of St Peter Mancroft Guild of Ringers, who have contributed half of this book.

The author acknowledges the financial support of Heart and the Harry Watson Bursary.

Maureen P Cubitt
August 2014

The Bells Told

Celebrating 300 years

St Peter Mancroft Guild of Ringers

CONTENTS

Part 1
A HISTORY

Introduction

On 2nd May 1715 the first recorded complete 'peal' was rung at St Peter Mancroft church in Norwich. It took three hours eighteen minutes, without stopping and without any bell rung out of place.

This book traces the history of the development of change ringing at Mancroft and looks to the future. There are many stories behind its former ringers; their ambitions, relationships, adventures, social life, successes and failures and rivalry between themselves and ringers from other towers. The reputation of the bells and Mancroft ringers in the early days influenced aspiring ringers in other parts of the country.

Members of the St Peter Mancroft Guild of Ringers today have their stories too and to this end members have contributed a piece from their experience and research. It is their vibrancy, enthusiasm, effort and commitment that make ringing at Mancroft so important. Although the history and heritage of our bells have their place, the future of ringing is more significant.

With the three hundredth anniversary of the first peal approaching in 2015, we would like to celebrate the achievement of 1715 with an ambitious project which would involve the creation of a Heritage and Training Centre in the tower. To make this possible, we would like to return the ringing chamber floor to its eighteenth century position, higher in the tower, thus creating a room beneath for displays and teaching. We hope to install eight 'dumb' bells there linked to computers and audio equipment. A Project Committee has been working on the plan for some time and we hope that some part of it will be underway by 2015.

Norwich is a centre of tourism and St Peter Mancroft is in the heart of the city. Our bells are known internationally in the ringing world, so we want to develop an out-reach programme to publicise the heritage, knowledge and skills of bell ringing to the general public as well as to ringers and to make our tower welcoming.

1
Voices of the Bells

St Peter Mancroft church, one of the finest medieval churches in England, stands at the centre of the city of Norwich. In medieval times Norwich was the second city after London. In terms of the English tradition of change ringing, it was the first.

In the fifteenth century the present church superseded the old Norman building. Of the four bells in the tower, one had probably hung in the former church and the others, cast at the Brasyer family's foundry in St Stephens's parish, were possibly cast in 1454 when money was received for new bell ropes. The church was completed the following year. About 1534 a further heavier bell was given by William Ellis, Baron of the Exchequer. These five rang for national and local events such as the anniversary of the coronation of Queen Elizabeth I, for her birthday and after the defeat of the Armada. From 1581 they rang annually for what they deemed the Commotion Day, referring back to Kett's Rebellion of 1549. On this anniversary the inhabitants of Norwich were obliged to shut up their shops and assemble at their parish church by seven in the morning for a service of thanksgiving for the deliverance of the city. Afterwards every church was commanded to toll their bells as the parishioners returned to their homes and occupations.

The ringers at Mancroft would have climbed the same spiral stone staircase that we do today, but in those earlier days, the way they rang was different. The old bells were only able to be chimed, so ringers pulled the ropes in random order. However, the uniquely English method of full circle change ringing gradually evolved after the Reformation. Churchwardens' accounts for St Peter Mancroft between 1583 and 1586 record work on the bells. During that period the 2nd was rehung and given a new wheel, the 3rd was fitted with a stay and wheel, several new clappers were cast and all the bells were repaired. It appears that at least some bells were rung with more control and that change ringing was beginning. The church clock also had a bell and the clock case protruded into the north side of the ringing chamber. A new clock was installed in 1582. In 1598 the top of the steeple was mended for 2s 4d, the stone mason installed the west window for 30s and his workman glazed it for 16s 8d. In 1600 all the bells were fitted with baldrics (leather straps to hold the clappers) and one received a new wheel. Two years later the Churchwardens' accounts record: 'Item pd to Dymond the carpenter for workmanship done by him about the hanging of the bells and for timber besides the xx of September 1602 as appeareth by his bill xx s.' and 'Item paid to William Brand bellfounder the xxj of April 1603 for the makying of a new bell now hanging in a frame in the steeple as appeareth by his bill xviij Li'. The spiral stairs were mended and new bell ropes were purchased. John Newton, the smith, mended clappers for the 2nd, 4th, 5th and the great bell in 1604. Possibly the bells, fitted with wheels, were adapted for change ringing.

St Peter Mancroft from the south. A drawing by Joseph Stannard (1797-1830)

Queen Elizabeth I died in 1603 and the bells proclaimed the crowning of James I. Judging by the repairs, particularly to the great bell, the ringers were regularly climbing the steeple stairs. It was the sexton's duty to toll this great bell after a death in the parish, generally for a fee of a shilling. It was also rung for sermons and solemn occasions. Further work was done on the tower and the steeple window in 1608, but ringing was unaffected. St Peter Mancroft was the traditional focus for civic celebrations, enabling the voices of the bells to mingle with the sounds of festivities. At that time events generally included the monarch's birthday, coronation anniversaries, royal births, Gunpowder Plot after 1605, feast days and Guild Day when the new mayor was proclaimed. In 1611, when Thomas Anguish was made mayor, a large crowd gathered to witness fireworks and several people were crushed to death. After that, fireworks were banned from this event and they had to make do with the sound of the bells.

In 1618/1619, £22 was received towards payment for bell metal. This was doubtless for the recasting of the tenor bell, inscribed 'Ego sum campana Gulielmi Ells baronis de exchequer que fracta refecta est 1618'. Work in the churchyard began in 1630. The great earthen bank around the perimeter was levelled and replaced with 72 yards of walling. Two years later a workman was paid 10s for mending the wall after it fell down! Loads of stone and lime were brought in to pave the alleys through the yard, two bell clappers were mended, a new rope was purchased and the ringers were paid 2s to ring for the new assistant minister, the Revd John Carter, who was to have a significant effect on the church and city during the Civil War.

In 1640, £10 3s was spent on repairs after a heavy stone apparently fell from the tower through the aisle roof. After that year, ringing had more of a political significance.

The Revd John Carter, a staunch Puritan, had been promoted to parish chaplain against the wishes of the king in 1638. So began a policy of zealously removing or destroying objects within the church deemed to be idolatrous. Images on the font were removed in 1642, although one was missed. The whole was then plastered with lime and daubed with black paint. Later the cross was removed from the steeple. Many objects were burnt in the market place including religious paintings. Two brass eagles and the organ were sold. Norwich was essentially a Puritan city; but, interestingly, the bells were not silenced during the Civil War; they were obviously needed to proclaim news:

>1639 Ringing for the peace with Scotland 5s and on the mayor's command upon the agreement between king and parliament 5s 6d.
>
>1645 July 26th at good news from Bridgewater 7s 6d.
>
>1645 Upon victory at Nasby 5s and victory against Goringe 7s 6d.
>
>1648 Upon the surrender of Colchester and routing the Scottish army 8s.

In 1648 a mob protesting against the arrest of the Royalist mayor of Norwich assembled in Chapelfield and accidentally fired 98 barrels of gunpowder stored in the committee house, causing severe damage to the windows of St Peter's and St Stephen's churches. As it could have been much worse, Bubbins the sexton was paid 7s 6d on 24th April for ringing for 'delivery from the Blow'. The east window was boarded up shortly afterwards by workmen who were paid in bread and beer. The glazier claimed £12 in July 1649. In 1651 the window was covered with a cloth that was apparently torn later and then replaced with sail cloth. Reglazing finally took place in 1652 at a cost of £55. Between 1655 and 1656 further work was done in the belfry, a new wheel was made for the 5th, and repairs made to all bells. In 1657 the ringers rang on the day the Lord Protector was proclaimed and three years later they pealed for the return of Charles II. After the restoration of the monarchy they were employed more often and the bells were a regular expense to the church, mostly for wheels, clappers, new ropes oil and grease. The Churchwardens' accounts of 1665 record that six mats were provided for the ropes to fall upon followed by a list:

	£	s	d
1666-7 Paid Brand for boring the greate bell when the cannons broke	2	0	0
1672-3 Received from the Reparation Rate and for the two new bells	93	8	6
Recd off Mr John Hobart as a gift towards the 2 new bells	3	0	0
Recd off Mr John Melchior as a gift towards the two new bells	0	10	0
Payd Edward Tooke for the mettall of the two new bells weighing 9 c 2qs 25 at 12d p lb.	54	0	0
Payd Edward Tooke for 4 brasses for the bells and mending the brasses for the ould second	1	13	4

£39 was paid for the chimes and quarters to Thomas Doo.

The inscriptions of these old bells were recorded by Benjamin Mackerell in 1736:

Treble	Edward Tooke made me anno domini 1675
2nd	Edward Tooke made me anno domini 1676
3rd	Anno Domini 1602
4th	Nos Thome meritis mereamur gaudia lucis
5th	Petrus ad eterne ducat nos paseua vite
6th	Ave Maria gracia plena dominus tecum
7th	Sum rosa pulsate mundi maria vocata
Tenor	Ego sum campana Gulielmi Elys baronis de Exchequer que fracta refecta est 1618

Repairs to the 4th and 7th bells in 1675 cost £2 10s, but Edward Tooke did not receive payment until 1679.

By this time the mathematics of change ringing had developed beyond simple permutations. With eight bells in the tower the ringers were ready to improve the skills that would make them and Mancroft's tower famous.

2
The First Peal Ever

Twenty pounds was spent on repairs to the bells in 1680 and the following year the first record appears of ringing in the New Year. The annual perambulation of the parish boundary was another day of celebration. In 1698, as well as payment for ringers, the church spent 24s on a barrel of beer, 20s on cake, 3s 6d on tobacco, £2 8s on the boys' beer and £10 3d on a grand dinner with wine for those involved.

A new organ was installed on a gallery at the west end of the church in 1707 and the space surrounding it boarded up. The upper part, as seen from the nave, contained a representation of a stained glass window. At that time the choir sang from the gallery. The ringing chamber floor was about half way up the west window.

Ringers were not in the job purely for payment; change ringing had become a mathematical challenge. Change ringing had been practised, probably ever since bells were fitted with wheels. The challenge was how to ring for as long as possible without repetition of the order. On seven bells, all the possible permutations is $1 \times 2 \times 3 \times 4 \times 5 \times 6 \times 7$ equalling 5040. It was reckoned that ringing all these changes would take about three and a half hours, so an achievable goal which became known as a peal. As there were eight bells in the tower, the heaviest bell, which was not involved in the changes on seven, would ring last to keep the rhythm. Of course, the Norwich ringers were not the only ones seeking this ultimate goal, London ringers were also in the contest. We know the Norwich ringers experimented by ringing half a peal in 1710 and there were at least two previous attempts at a complete peal, but these were discounted as there was a repetition of changes.

A number of ringers at Mancroft were worstead weavers, including John Garthon, who was admitted a freeman of Norwich in 1693. Perhaps seated at his loom making cloth, he conceived the way of 'weaving' the path of seven bells to arrive at 5040 variations without a repetition; for it was he who solved the problem. On 2nd May 1715 John Garthon and his fellow ringers achieved the first peal in 3 hours and 18 minutes. It was recorded on a board that still hangs in the ringing chamber. It was called Grandsir(e) Bob which today is called Plain Bob. John Garthon died in 1728 and was buried at St Gregory's, Norwich.

The 1715 Peal Board

The Norwich ringers next succeeded in ringing the first peal of Grandsire Triples, a method rung regularly in towers today:

On the 26th of August: 1718 was Rung that Harmonious Peal Called Grandsire Triples, which have been ye study of ye most Ingenious men of this Age, who delight in ye art of Variations, but all their Projections have proved errors untill it was undertook by JOHN GARTHON who with long Study and Practice have perfectly discovered those Intricate methods which were hidden from the eyes of all the Ringers in England: the extent of this Peal being 5040 Changes have often times been Rung with Changes alike, but the first time that ever it was Rung true was in three hours and a half, without any Changes alike or a Bell out of Course by these men whose names are under written against their Bells as they Rung.

James Brook	Treble	Henry Howard	5th
John Briggs	2nd	Wm Callow	6th
Wm Palmer	3rd	Tho. Melchior	7th
Robt Crane	4th	Tho. Barrett	Tenor

Although John Garthon was the composer, this time he did not ring. Of the ringers who did not ring in the 1715 peal, Robert Crane was an alehouse keeper, Henry Howard was a worstead weaver and William Callow kept the inn called Labour-in-Vain.

On 28th December 1719, a third peal was rung, another of Grandsire Triples, but only names of the ringers of 6th, 7th and 8th are recorded. The conductor of the peal, Thomas Melchior, did not report the peal until much later, writing in the *Norwich Gazette* on 20th November 1731 stating that stating 'the other bells my domestic adversaries rung'!

These ringers were all members of the Norwich Scholars. The name 'Scholars' or 'Youths' was a name incorporated in the names of many eighteenth century ringing societies. The Norwich Scholars were virtually indistinguishable from the names of members of the Norwich Ringers' Purse, established in 1716. 'Love as Brethren' was the motto shared by both societies, which from time to time both Scholars and Purse members aspired to with difficulty.

3
Ringing Rivalry

In 1726 the ring at St Michael's Coslany, was increased to eight. On 1st April 1727 a double peal of 10080 changes of Oxford Treble Bob Major was rung there by the Society of Norwich Ringers, taking 6 hours 28 minutes, which was the first ever double peal to be rung. It is thought that Garthon was the composer; Robert Crane, who rang in the peal of Grandsire at Mancroft, rang the seventh and was possibly the conductor, as his name alone is painted in capital letters on the peal board which hangs in the tower.

In 1729 the Norwich ringers were involved in a challenge by the ringers from Eye in Suffolk. The following advertisement appeared in the *Norwich Gazette* on Saturday 23rd August 1729:

'WHEREAS the Norwich Society of Ringers, have been challenged by the Ringers of Eye, in the county of Suffolk; this is to let them know, That we the said Norwich Ringers refuse none who challenge us to ring, at Five, Six, Seven or Eight Bells: And that We, whose Names are hereto subscribed, do accept the said Challenge of the Ringers of Eye aforesaid; and will ring with them for Ten Guineas, (who shall ring best, both for Variety and Truth) and meet then Half Way from their town, as near as a Peal will Serve: And we do moreover expect their Answer to this under their Hands, in Like Manner, in the same News-Paper, within 2 or 3 Saturday's at longest, or we shall look upon then as Nothing but Wind.

JOHN BRIGGS.	ROBERT CRANE.
THOMAS GARDINER.	RICHARD BARNHAM.
WILLIAM CALLOW.	THOMAS BARRET.
THOMAS MELCHIOR.	JOHN FORSTER.
JOHN HARVEY.	JOHN WEBSTER.
EDWARD CRANE.	&c. &c. &c. &c. &c.'

This list of names includes all those who rang in the long peal of Oxford Treble Bob Major. Following lengthy arguments in the newspaper, the Norwich ringers met with the Eye ringers at Bungay on 14th October. The Eye ringers later published that the Norwich ringers had refused to ring. Norwich ringers, angry with their advertisement, accused them of ringing a blundering peal or two then 'sneaking out of town in the dark, wisely preventing being hissed at by the people'. The *Norwich Gazette* recorded the wrangling which continued until the end of November, but the challenge was never resolved.

As time went on, Coslany and Mancroft ringers split into factions with the Crane family virtually in control of Coslany tower. They challenged Mancroft ringers to be the first to compose and ring a peal of Stedman Triples.

Stedman, a ringing principle discovered by Fabian Stedman, and popular today, was far more difficult than the basic methods practised at that time and had never been extended to a peal. Edward Crane claimed to have composed a peal of Stedman Triples, as reported in the *Gazette* on 11th September 1731. Any ringers wanting to challenge this achievement were invited to visit the Six Ringers Inn at St Michael's Coslany and take a bet on it from two guineas to ten. Hostilities had begun and the Mancroft band was stirred into action. Thomas Melchior, considered to be the leading ringer in Norwich, was not to sit still and let another usurp his position. However, the sixth bell at Mancroft was in a poor state whereas the Coslany bells were in better condition. About a month after Crane's challenge, Melchior declared that Stedman Triples had been composed by him and rung with seven others at St Peter Mancroft. The Coslany rivals must have been told about the peal attempt, for Thomas Crane and two others met at a local inn, perhaps the White Hart or White Horse, to count the blows of the tenor, not easy to concentrate for nearly four hours and it would have been thirsty work. They reckoned they counted only 4860 changes. Melchior retorted that they must have miscounted since they had been in a busy public house where people were often coming in and going out. He accused them of being false and malicious and felt it beneath him to reply to their insulting and scandalous words. The Mancroft success was published in the *Norwich Gazette* of 30th October 1731:

'NOT withstanding the Pretensions of several ingenious ringers in this City and elsewhere…this is thereforeto satisfie all Lovers of that ingenious Art That Thomas Melchior has composed it to Truth…being the First that ever was composed all perfect Stedman, consisting of 5040 changes: And was rung by him and 7 more on Monday 25th of October, 1731 at St. Peter's of Mancroft in Norwich, in 3 Hours and 40 Minutes; and never a Bell out of Course, nor changes alike: By us whose names are here subscribed viz:

Thomas Melchior,- Treble; Thomas Blofield, 2d; Wm. Palmer, 3d; Thomas Utber 4th; John Gardiner - 5th; John Foster - 6th; Christopher Beauty (sic)7th; William Porter, - Tenor.

NOTE.- If any of the Curious be desirous, they may see the Peal, at John Foster's at the sign of the Eight Bells in St Peter's of Mancroft aforesaid, and satisfie themselves without laying any Wager.'

The first round was won by Melchior and in due course a peal board was erected in the belfry at Mancroft. At the top of the board are the words SWEAR NOT AT ALL, followed by a poetic inscription:

> On the 25th of Octobr. 1731 here was Rung that Miste-
> rious Peal called Stedman Tripples the Discovery thereof have
> been the Study of several Ingenious Ringers in England —
> though to no Effect untill this Intricate Peal which differs from all
> other Methods of Tripples, as being every Bell alike course was perfectly
> Discoverd by Thos. Melchior who first compleated this Peal, all
> Perfect Stedman Tripples with only two doubles & no Alteration the
> Extent being 5040 Changes was Compleatly rang by us in 3
> hours & 40 minutes on which Occasion Willm. Scot in his remar
> upon the ringing this Peal did Elegantly sing. Viz. —
> As for the Sweet and Pleasent Treble. She
> by Melchior well was Rung that Bell & called the Bobs so Free.
> Blofield the 2d Palmer 3d did ring. —
> Ulber rang 4th & was not Loath, but made her for to Sing. —
> Gardener the 5th did sway. Foster the 6th did Play. —
> the 7th round Cris Buty bound, & made her to Obey —
> the Tenor fine & neat brave Porter so Compleat —
> did ring her out & turn'd about, that Cymbal loud & great.

The lower part of the Stedman peal board

Three hours forty minutes is quite a long time for a peal of triples. The tenor weighed 23cwt, so was not especially heavy. It could only mean that the bells were not going well and the 6th was particularly difficult.

John Webster had been present in the tower as referee during the peal to check Melchior's calling – and had been accused of being 'a Prompter as in a Play' and also of relieving John Foster, the ringer of the 6th. He swore to a magistrate later that it had been true, although on cross-examination he prevaricated somewhat.

A few years after this peal John Foster left, having deceitfully stolen the Purse book from the Company of Ringers. The magistrates fined him two marks at court in May 1737. He never rang a peal again with any of the Purse members and took himself off to Suffolk and from there to Lincolnshire, where he continued to practise the art of ringig. In 1756 he conducted a peal of Grandsire Triples in Lincoln to John Garthon's composition.

Melchior and the Mancroft band had rung their peal of Stedman, but that was not the end of the story. The Coslany ringers tried to obtain a copy of the peal composition but were fobbed off with a copy of an earlier attempt.

St Michael's Coslany ringers did achieve their peal on 6th December 1731 despite, they alleged, dubious tactics by their rivals, such as hiring a bell-man to shout scandalous verses, employing boys to throw stones at the church door and on to the roof and using a boy to attempt entry through a window, (he was prevented and sent home with a bloody nose) – all, of course, denied by the Mancroft men. Melchior accused Crane of calling the bobs from a piece of paper nailed up in the tower. Five years later, however, the bands were reconciled when a new challenge would unite them.

14

4
The Bloody Peal

It was unusual, in the early part of the eighteenth century outside London, for a tower to have a ring of more than eight bells. Not to be outdone by their London rivals, John Stephens, from Norwich, encouraged by ringers keen to take up the challenge of ringing on 10, cast two trebles in July 1724. The new bells were a good tone and it was generally believed they would satisfy all critics. When heard for the first time they were pronounced to be as good a ring of ten bells as any in England. Despite advertising, subscriptions were not forthcoming and the two trebles were removed in October. They were going to be broken up, but were first advertised in Norwich should other parishes be interested. It is not known if either were bought.

In 1736 the ring was again increased to ten, but shortly afterwards the two new bells were returned to London 'as not agreeable' and were replaced. When these new bells were hung, the remaining eight were overhauled and improvements made. The *Gazette* advertised on 26th June 1736 that 'on Tuesday next, at four in the afternoon, being St Peter's Day, the ten bells at St Peter's Church will be rung for the first time'.

Mancroft was thus confirmed as the leading ringing tower of Norwich. How could the ringers from other towers resist stretching their abilities? The first ten bell peal in Norfolk was rung at Aylsham in 1736. However, Mancroft reached a pinnacle of ringing achievement on 8th March 1738 with a peal of Grandsire Caters containing 12600 changes rung by nine men and two youths, the first of whom rang above 8000 changes, the other finished the peal. A board, high up in the ringing chamber, describes the peal as containing:

'Harmonious changes and ye Number of them was certainly superior to anything of its kind ever done in the World and to Remove all doubt of the truth of the performance, several ingenious Ringers were abroad the whole time with proper Rules to prove the certainty of the same, thus this great Peal was perfectly completed to the entire satisfaction, surprise and Amazement of thousands of hearers which they completed in 8 hours 15 minutes, the greatest number of changes that was ever rung hereto in England.'

Eight of the band had rung in one or other of the Stedman peals. Now they stood shoulder to shoulder:

Thomas Melchior	Treble	*Mancroft*	William Porter	6th	*Mancroft*
William Pettingall	2nd	*Coslany*	Thomas Blofield	7th	*Mancroft*
John Gardiner	3rd	*Mancroft*	Edward Crane	8th	*Coslany*
Thomas Barrett	4th	*Mancroft*	Christopher Booty	9th	*Mancroft*
Robert Crane	5th	*Coslany*	Robert Lyddiman	} Tenor	
			James Jarom		

The peal board records the date by the Julian calendar. Under this system, the New Year began on 25th March. The Norwich Gazette used the Gregorian calendar with 1st January as the start of the year. The Gregorian calendar was adopted nationally in 1752.

This peal was known as the 'Bloody Peal' owing to the state of the ringers' hands at the end. Not all members of the rival Stedman bands could be in this peal. Thomas Crane did not join his father and brother. Perhaps he had not forgiven Melchior or was considered not good enough, his friend Richard Greene was also missing. Neither composer nor conductor are mentioned, perhaps a matter of diplomacy. It remained the longest ten bell peal for 151 years.

Left: the peal board as it appears in the Ninham painting c.1850 (The peal board next to it in the foreground records two peals of 1775 and 1778)

Right: The handsome long-length peal board still hangs in its lofty position.

A new peal of ten bells was hung at Stonham Aspal, Suffolk, in 1743 and Mancroft ringers were invited to try them out. Norwich and Aylsham ringers even hired lodgings at Stonham Magpie Inn, in order to be there early in the morning. On 16th July the *Ipswich Journal* reported:

'THIS is to inform the GENTLEMEN in the County of Suffolk, or elsewhere, that are Lovers of the Art of Ringing, that the Old Practitioners of St Peter's of Mancroft in the City of Norwich, are fully determin'd, God willing, to be at Aspal Stonham in Suffolk, the 28th Instant at Night, in order on the 29th to attempt to Ring some curious Peals… by your humble servants Melchior, Webster, Crane and the Ringers aforesaid.

N.B. We shall begin at Nine o'Clock in the Morning of the same Day.'

It was a time when new recruits were encouraged. On Monday 1st February 1748 a peal of Oxford Treble Bob Major was rung at Mancroft by a young company in 3 hours 26 minutes. In April 1754 Mancroft ringers opened the new ring of eight at East Dereham in Norfolk. Eight of the youngest ringers in Norwich rang a peal of Double Court Bob Major at St Giles' in 1755.

Events such as this were probably celebrated not just in the local hostelries, but in the ringing chamber. In 1749 a large pot or gotch was given by John Dersley to the Mancroft ringers and was certainly used annually on New Year's Eves.

The Ringers' Jug

Thomas Melchior was now the accepted leading ringer of Norwich. He died in 1755 and was buried at St John Maddermarket. During his life he was nicknamed 'copperfaced Melchior', perhaps because members of his family were coppersmiths, or maybe his complexion.

John Webster had remained a prominent member of the Norwich Scholars. Around 1753, John Cundell of the College Youths proposed to publish John Holt's compositions of Triples in a broadsheet. The Revd Charles Mason of Cambridge wrote to Webster to solicit support from the Norwich ringers. Webster indicated that since Benjamin Annable (a prominent London ringer) did not approve of the publication there was not likely to be any support for the proposal from the Norwich company. When the broadsheet was published nobody from Norwich had subscribed. John Webster met his death in St Giles' church tower on 17th November 1760 having just completed a peal. A stone tablet records:

'Near to this Place JOHN WEBSTER fell
Belov'd by all that knew him well;
The most Ingenious noted Ringer
S^t. Giles's sixth Bell around did bring Her;
He clos'd the Peal struck well his Bell,
Ceasing the same, down Dead. 'He fell.'"

The *Norwich Mercury* of Saturday 22nd November 1760 noted his passing:

'On Monday last died in the St. Giles's Steeple, John Webster, a noted and ingenious Ringer, an honest, sober and industrious Man, respected and esteem'd by all his Acquaintance, the Peal he had been ringing of, prov'd his farewell one, for he ended that and Life together: He kept his Bell in due Order to the close of the Cease, then fell and rose no more.'

He had been a member of the Norwich Ringers' Purse, receiving sickness payments in 1745, 1749, 1753 and 1759. The Purse made a burial grant on the day of his funeral.

Of the other ringers, William Pettingall cast hand bells in the 1750s at the Shuttle and Hand-Bell near St Lawrence's Steps and later kept a shop, the Ringers' Arms, in the same area. It was burgled in 1779, a quantity of meat stolen and he died very shortly afterwards. Thomas Barrett was a worstead weaver. His name was crossed out of the Purse Book in 1742 for receiving money fraudulently. Robert Crane kept an alehouse. Edward Crane, who composed the Coslany peal of Stedman, was clerk of St Gregory's parish for 46 years. He died in 1774 aged 73. No more peal boards were put up at Mancroft for forty years until 1778. Thus a noted ringer, John Chamberlin, who had died in 1773, does not appear. He conducted several significant peals and was a great traveller.

5
The Travelling Company

Norwich in the eighteenth century, except where bounded by the river, was surrounded by medieval walls with gates that shut at eight o'clock in the evening. However, modernity was on its way when in 1771 streets signs were erected and a new obelisk fitted with lamps illuminated the market place. That year it was reported that two drunken fellows on horseback had ridden furiously through the streets of the city with sticks, destroying about thirty lamps. An accident in the market in 1778, however, was probably appreciated when a wagon from Stowmarket crashed carrying 300 half ankers of gin. Only 40 were saved!

Very close to the west end of the tower stood the White Swan, a large inn patronised by the county gentry and home of the Norwich Company of Comedians. Performances generally began at 7pm the doors opening at 5pm. The gentry would send their servants at 4pm to keep seats. The lower boxes were the most fashionable priced at 2s 6d, next to them the pit at 2s. The upper boxes and front gallery came at 1s 6d and 1s. The vulgar herd had limited standing at 6d a head.

This was the world of the Norwich ringers where St Peter Mancroft continued to be a centre of excellence inspiring both the experienced and the young. William Porter, a long-standing member of the band, composed the method called Norwich Court Bob Royal in 1751 and a peal of it was rung in 1769. Many years later in 1816, it was rung in London as Court Bob Royal and claimed as a first. (Norwich ringers were incensed!) He was a trunk maker who lived in Cockey Lane and had a shop in the Market place. Hand bells, belonging to the Norwich Scholars were kept in a leather trunk made by Porter. He died in 1770. The trunk still existed in the 1920s.

The young company of ringers clearly wanted to ring in towers other than Norwich. Eight of them rang a peal of 5040 Court Bob Major at North Elmham on 19th January 1758, apparently the first time it was rung in England. The peal was conducted by John Chamberlin, an adventurous man, whose growing reputation and that of his fellow ringers, would enhance the fame of St Peter Mancroft ringers.

They may have heard of an advertisement placed by Samuel Turner, bell-hanger for Lester and Pack, of Whitechapel, in the *York Courant* inviting ringers to open the new ring of bells at York Minster on 19th August 1765. Many years later, an article in The Salopian Journal of 12th October 1808, in a collection by Samuel Lawrence of Shifnal states: 'The Peal of Ten Bells of York Minster, were cast by Lester and Pack in 1765, and opened by Ringers from St. Peter's Mancroft, Norwich, on the Prince of Wales' Birthday, August 12th 1765, who Rang on them 1,600 Bob Royals'. John Eisel, in his booklet The Gothic Traveller, suggests this article may have been written by John Parnell. Parnell, Samuel Lawrence and Robert Chesnutt from Norwich, were all prominent members of the Ancient Society of College Youths. Certainly bells were rung on the Prince of Wales' birthday during the celebrations, as it was reported in the *York Courant*.

John Chamberlin and his fellow ringers were invited to open the new eight bells at St Nicholas', King's Lynn with a peal of Bob Major on 20th November 1766. On the 28th October 1770 they were at Great Yarmouth to ring a peal of Bob Major. They had not intended to publish the fact, but were taunted by some Suffolk ringers, who declared that Norwich Ringers could not manage to ring a peal in any steeple where the bells were heavy.

In 1771, eight of the band undertook a more extensive ringing tour ringing a peal of Bob Major at Downham Market on Sunday 23rd June, the first on the bells and another first on the bells at Wisbech in the Isle of Ely the following day. The same band rang each time and both peals were conducted by John Chamberlin:

John Chamberlin	Treble	Simon Watling	5th
John Keepus	2nd	John Dye	6th
John Dixon	3rd	John Trowse	7th
James Watling	4th	James Vines	Tenor

On 26th June they opened a new peal of eight at Holbeach in Lincolnshire and many locals came to listen. The same company went to Coltishall on Monday 1st July, and rang for hats, which they won. (It was quite common for hats to be a reward for winning a ringing competition.) Clues from their itinerary may indicate how they travelled:

15th June	St Michael Coslany, Norwich - a peal of 6720 Court Bob
23rd June	Downham Market - a peal of 5040 Bob Major
24th June	Wisbech - a peal of 5040 Bob Major
26th June	Holbeach - a peal of Bob Major
1st July	Coltishall - a ringing competition

It would be quite possible to walk the forty odd miles from Norwich to Downham via Dereham and Swaffham for the 23rd June. Rather tougher to ring a peal at Downham then walk over four hours the next day to Wisbech to ring another peal. They may have hitched a lift to speed their progress from time to time, but it is likely that most of the journey would have been done on foot. In 1772, they were yet more ambitious. The *Leicester and Nottingham Journal*, recorded the adventurous Norwich ringers in their paper the 25th July:

'Last week a company of Change-ringers in the city of Norwich, arrived at home from a tour into the north of England, after having taken a circuit of upwards of four hundred miles, in which they visited the cities of Lincoln and York, and most of the principal towns in those parts, where they were treated with the greatest respect and in the politest manner, and were much admired for their skill in the ingenious art of Campanology. Amongst their performances was a 5040, Eight In, rang at Holbeach in Lincolnshire, where their names with the bell that each rang was put up in the belfry. They intended to have touched at Nottingham and Leicester in their return from York, had they not been detained in that city longer than they expected'.

One is left wondering how these far from wealthy men could afford to make these excursions and what detained them at York. Perhaps on their return, the ringers made enquiries about new bells for Norwich to match those of York, for on 20th November 1772 a letter was printed, encouraging Norwich inhabitants to provide new bells.

About three months later they lost John Chamberlin, their leader and the inspiration for the travelling company. The *Norfolk Chronicle* reported on Saturday 6th February 1773 'Tuesday last died, much regretted, that most ingenious Ringer, John Chamberlin, one of the company belonging to St Peter's of Mancroft, an honest and industrious man, who was remarkable for his extensive knowledge both in the theory and practice of the art of Ringing'.

Finally the influential population of Norfolk and Norwich felt the county deserved better, after all the Mancroft ringers had been treated with the fame of today's football heroes; it was only fitting that they should be given the best bells on which to practise their art. It was also a matter of civic pride. The second bell was cracked and useless, the sixth increasingly difficult and some of the others almost worn out.

St Peter Mancroft and the Market Place c.1830
(Image courtesy of Norfolk County Council Library and Information Service)

6
The Royal Twelve

The eighteenth century is considered the age of enlightenment with the development of scientific, intellectual and cultural interests. Change ringing was just one of the fascinations.

Mancroft was at the centre of the city. As the bells rang out folk would gather in the market place, a large space when the market was not operating, to enjoy whatever entertainment was on offer. When Norwich was celebrating, the militia generally fired a round or two; often a grand procession of dignitaries took place with illuminations in the evening. The newspapers summarized such occasions as observed with 'the usual demonstrations of joy.' On Guild Day, for example, churches were adorned with streamers and streets decorated with flags.

A new era for ringing in Norwich was approaching with an advertisement in the *Norwich Mercury* on 8th October 1774 announcing the launch of the appeal for twelve new bells. A fortnight later a correspondent pointed out the benefits to shopkeepers and inn keepers from the increase of visitors to the city. In February 1775, an anonymous song, to the tune of Wilkes's Wriggle, was published in the Norfolk Chronicle, of which just a verse or two here:

Ye Bucks and Wits and square-toe'd Cits
Of Norwich, gallant City,
Ye Country Squires and Knights of Shires
Come harken to our Ditty.
What furious Zeal and Storms assail
Us BELLES of Great Saint Peter's;
Like ragged Whores, turn'd out of Doors;
Alas; unhappy Creatures!

Church wardens tell, that Sister NELL
Has crack'd her Constitution;
But we declare they Bunglers are,
Unfit for Execution;
Full of the Great in Church and State
Have quarrelled to ingage Her,
If conqu'ring Wight advance'd in fight,
She tipt him the Bob Major.

Then why should we, insulted be
With language coarse and scurvy,
For pleasing those, who oft have chose
To turn us topsy-turvy;
Or how they dare presume to say
We much of Merit lack Sirs.
For having what most BELLES have got
An inoffensive CRACK Sirs.

Then hear our Prayer and kindly spare
Such BELLES from tribulation,
What shame 'twou'd be such stuff to see
Dissolv'd by Salivation;
But should ill will pursue us still
And Malice know no bound'ry
Then in the lurch, we'll leave the Church
To sorrow in the Found'ry.

A week later the response came: For the NORFOLK CHRONICLE Spoken Extempore on reading the Verses in your last Paper.

> Tis thought you never wrote before
> Nay 'faith your verses shew it;
> Then be advis'd and write no more'
> You'll never be a poet.
>
> Perhaps you read with Rapture o'r
> The Nonsense that you writ
> But pray forbear and write no more
> You'll never be a Wit.

The estimated cost of a new peal of twelve was £600 excluding old materials. It was to be nearly double that figure. The project was well advertised and soon local dignitaries took an interest. In November it was reported that Sir Harbord Harbord had subscribed £50 and Sir Edward Astley, Bart and Wenman Coke Esq had contributed 30 guineas each, the parishioners almost £200. The *Norwich Mercury* on 26th November pointed out that there had never been a peal of twelve bells cast all at the same time. A list of subscribers of £5 and more was published. No Norwich ringer's name appears, so they may have banded together for a group donation.

	£	s	d
Weight of ye peal 183. 2. 24 at £6 per cwt	1102	5	8½
12 clappers 3. 3. 3 at 9d per lb	15	19	6
To Wharfage Landing etc of the old bells	3	0	6
To Wharfage of the new bells	4	13	6
To Samuel Turner for the new Oak Frame, Gudgeons, Screws, Hanging the Bells as by agreement	113	0	0
	1238	19	2½

Early in 1775 the 'inharmonious and ruinous' set of bells was removed from the tower. Seven of the old bells were shipped to London and two sold to Bungay. The new bells, cast by Pack and Chapman at Whitechapel, arrived from London, by wherry, on Wednesday 3rd June 1775 and were conveyed to the tower the following day. They were deemed to be as melodious as any in the kingdom, said to be in the key of C, but tuned with the temperament of the E flat scale, which gave them a distinctive and rather melancholy quality. They were named The Royal Twelve.

Details of the inscriptions and weights of the bells:

Bell	Inscription	Weight
Treble	PACK & CHAPMAN OF LONDON FECIT 1775 / TO THE COMMON COUNCIL WHO GAVE 50 GUINEAS THIS BELL IS INSCRIB'D	6-3-5
2nd	PACK & CHAPMAN OF LONDON FECIT 1775 / ST PETER MANCROFT RICHD. FORSTER THOS. COLE CHURCHWARDENS 1775	6-2-15
3rd	PACK & CHAPMAN OF LONDON FECIT 1775 / THE REVD. JNO PEELE THE REVD THOS. NICHOLS MINISTERS	6-3-20
4th	PACK & CHAPMAN OF LONDON FECIT 1775 / ROGER KERRISON ESQR SHERIFF AND AN ALDERMAN OF THIS WARD	7-3-8
5th	PACK & CHAPMAN OF LONDON FECIT 1775 / CHARLES WESTON ESQR ALDERMAN OF THIS WARD	9-0-5
6th	PACK & CHAPMAN OF LONDON FECIT 1775 / THOS STARLING ESQR ALDERMAN OF THIS WARD	9-3-19
7th	PACK & CHAPMAN OF LONDON FECIT 1775 / SR. THOS. CHURCHMAN KT. ALDERMAN OF THIS WARD	11-2-7
8th	PACK & CHAPMAN OF LONDON FECIT 1775 / JOHN LORD HOBART SON AND HEIR APPARENT OF JOHN EARL OF BUCKM.	14-0-18
9th	PACK & CHAPMAN OF LONDON FECIT 1775 / WENMAN COKE ESQR. REPRESENTATIVE FOR NORFOLK GAVE 30 GUINEAS	19-1-27
10th	PACK & CHAPMAN OF LONDON FECIT 1775 / SIR EDWARD ASTLEY BART. REPRESENTATIVE FOR NORFOLK GAVE 30 GUINEAS	21-3-6
11th	PACK & CHAPMAN OF LONDON FECIT 1775 / SIR HARBORD HARBORD BART. REPRESENTATIVE FOR NORFOLK AND ALDERMAN GAVE FIFTY POUNDS	28-2-2
Tenor	PACK & CHAPMAN OF LONDON FECIT 1775 / TO KING QUEEN AND THEIR TEN CHILDREN THIS HARMONIOUS PEAL OF TWELVE BELLS IS DEDICATED	43-1-19

The 1775 frame photographed c.1900

Tickets for the opening of the bells on St Peter's day, 21ˢᵗ June 1775, with a Grand Te Deum and Jubilate, a chorus from the Messiah and the Coronation Anthem, were obtainable at the Coffee House, King's Head in the Market, the White Swan, the Maid's Head, the New Inn, the Rose Tavern, the Rampant Horse and the King's Head in Magdalen Street. Performers included thirty gentlemen accompanied by the voices of the Cathedral choir who were treated afterwards to dinner with the ringers by the churchwardens. The churchwardens' accounts record a bill for £1 13s 0d for feeding the ringers at King's Head and for their ringing. The singers bill was for £2 18s 6d and cleaning the church afterwards cost 14s.

The first peal on the new bells, 5170 Grandsire Cinques, was rung on Wednesday 22ⁿᵈ November 1775. It was declared that not one bell was out of its proper course in the space of four hours one minute to the surprise of all listeners because of the difficulty of the performance and especially as it was done at the first attempt. Gentlemen who had not subscribed to the new bells were strongly rebuked. Thomas Barton, ringer of the fifth, was still ringing until his death in 1821 aged 92. He was the oldest ringer at Mancroft at that time.

The ringers announced in the *Norfolk Chronicle* that, obviously, parishioners would prefer the sound of bells to the absurd, uncivilized, custom of playing instruments after midnight in the run up to Christmas, apparently disturbing sleeping children, enraging musicians and causing pregnant women to give birth before their time! They thanked all those who had provided the new bells and promised to entertain the public by ringing two evenings in every week during Advent.

Towards the latter part of the eighteenth century, the popularity of long-length peal ringing increased and rivalry developed between London-based societies, the Ancient Society of College Youths and the Society of Royal Cumberland Youths. In 1778, Mancroft ringers, who were all members of the Cumberlands, rang 6240 Oxford Treble Bob Maximus on the 16th March in 5 hours 22 minutes, declaring that it excelled every other attempt hitherto known upon twelve bells in England:

Thomas Barton	Treble	John Dixon	7th
John Peak	2nd	James Watling	8th
John Havers	3rd	Simon Watling	9th
William Warner	4th	John Dye	10th
John Read	5th	James Vines	11th
Christopher Lindsey	6th	John and James Trowse	Tenor

Conducted by Thomas Barton

In 1785, the reputation of the Norwich Scholars and the fine ring of twelve at Mancroft encouraged some College Youths from London to pay a visit. When making their arrangements they had not said that they intended to attempt a peal. However, one of the London ringers, Christopher Wells, told the Norwich men that they were going to have an attempt for the Treble Bob Maximus record:

'This news created such ill feeling, that the Norwich Company refused to associate with them until an apology, and a satisfactory explanation was given, after which they were friendly and rang together. – The College Youths however ascended the Steeple and with a decided intention to beat the Norwich peal if at all possible, but in this they failed after ringing about a thousand changes.'

Shortly after this the Norwich ringers demonstrated their ability to ring a touch of Stedman Cinques. This really impressed the visitors. William Jones, John Reeves and Thomas Blakemore from London were collecting material for a book on change ringing and nowhere outside London were there so many methods rung. However, Christopher Lindsey and Thomas Barton, from Norwich were thinking about producing a book themselves and had no intention of giving away any secrets. A plan was forged and the Londoners asked if one of their company could stay on at Norwich for a while to learn Stedman Cinques in order to teach the others. Thomas Blakemore was an obvious choice as he had been to Norwich in 1777. He lodged with Christopher Lindsay for several months and apparently secretly made copies of his host's papers. The book Clavis Campanalogia was published without acknowledging the work of Norwich ringers. When the book appeared, not a single Norwich man had subscribed to it.

Not surprisingly, another visit to Norwich in 1789 was not particularly welcomed. Unfortunately the *Norfolk Chronicle* reported that the best London ringers had been chosen in order to contest the abilities of the Mancroft ringers. Matters had got off to a bad start! The visitors were not received very cordially as the Norwich men felt threatened. It was not a successful encounter between 'the rival sons of the clapper', tempers were frayed, there were arguments and the Londoners departed in disgust.

St Peter Mancroft from the Market Place before the restoration
(Image courtesy of Norfolk County Council Library and Information Service)

7
Battle of the Beefsteaks

Many ringers in the eighteenth century were employed in more than one job and considered ringing to be one of them. Most payments came from the civic authorities and from individuals who wanted bells rung for personal reasons, weddings, for example, but sometimes the church paid them in porter and beer like the women who cleaned the church and the man who tended the church clock. The method of payment sometimes involved ringing for half the time, collecting money from the sponsor and then ringing again.

Ringers at that time were not permitted to ring without permission of the wardens except on festival days. For example, in August 1729, the *Norwich Gazette* reported that after ringing for a sheriff elect and returning to the tower after part payment, they were prevented by the orders of a churchwarden. Undeterred, they went back to the sheriff's house and entertained him with handbells.

In 1775 the friendly society, the Purse, spent £4 8s 6d on the Christmas meeting and their tankards were engraved at a cost of 16s. Churchwardens' accounts of 1782 show they spent 6s 6d on greasing the bells and it was agreed that there would be no ringing of bells on any public day at the expensive of the church.

A list of payments for ringing exists from 1785-1800, recording the dates when ringers were paid by the civic authorities or by individuals. No ringers' salary is included. An example for 1778 follows:

		£	s	d
Jan 1st	New Year's Day		1	10
Jan 18th	Queen's Birthday	2	2	0
Jan 19th	The Right Hon. William Windham	2	2	0
Feb 23rd	Rev. Mr Waller to Miss…	1	1	0
Mar 18th	Mr J Roach elected	1	1	0
Mar 28th	Easter Monday	1	1	0
April 12th	Twist Esq. to Miss Scott wedding		7	6
May 1st	Elias Norgate elected mayor	2	2	0
May 10th	Rev Mr Beckwith to …	2	2	0
May 16th	Whitson Monday	1	1	0
May 19th	Mr Barber wine merchant to Miss…	3	3	0
May 27th	Mr D Martinue to Miss…	2	2	0
May 31st	Earl of Orford	2	2	0
June 1st	Mr Decker ascending Air Balloon	2	2	0
June 4th	King's birthday	2	2	0
June 24th	Guild Day	3	3	0
June 22nd	Mr Decker 2nd ascension	1	1	0
June 23rd	Mr Coldham to Miss…	1	1	0

Date	Event			
June 29th	St Peters' Day	1	1	0
July 15th	Sir John Wodehouse	1	1	0
July 10th	Assizes	12	12	0
July 26th	Mr Payne to Miss Bensell	2	2	0
Aug 12th	George Prince of Wales' Birthday	2	2	0
Aug 14th	Mr Charles Man to Miss…		10	6
Aug 18th	…Donne Surgeon to Miss Robinson	3	3	0
Aug 24th	Sir Edward Ashley	1	1	0
Aug 30th	Aldn. J Patteson Elected Sherriff	3	3	0
Sep 6th	Mr Smith to Miss Church	2	2	0
Sep 22nd	Coronation	2	2	0
Sep 29th	…	2	12	0
Oct 25th	King's Ascension	2	2	0
Nov 5th	Gun Powder Plot	2	2	0
Nov 28th	Mr Bullen to Miss Williams	2	2	0
Nov 30th	Mr …	2	12	6
Dec 5th	…	1	1	0
Dec 6th	Mr Carver to Miss Troughton	1	1	0
Dec 26th	Offering	16	3	0
Dec 31st	Captain Lodington to Miss Shouldham	3	3	0
		96	6	6

In 1794, the *Norfolk Chronicle* reported that fraudsters had been taking payment. The ringers gratefully thanked the nobility and gentry for their services, but cautioned them against impostors, who had pretended to be from Mancroft although some of them belonged to St Stephen's where there was only one bell and others from St Giles', where the bells were not permitted to ring. To guard against the swindlers, the ringers asked that future application should be by letter, sealed in the inside with a motto and the city arms.

Ringing for the Assizes and the 'Offering' (Boxing Day) were by far the most lucrative. Money was not brought conveniently to them in an envelope; it had to be collected. On Offering Day 1808 the ringers divided into three groups, to speed the collections of money and agreed to meet at the sign of the New Theatre in Bethel Street at noon for a feast of beef steak and a few draughts of porter before going back to ring.

The food was prepared and waiting for the ringers; but greedy scoundrels seated in the kitchen had spotted the savoury feast and decided to attack. However, at this point, the first party of ringers arrived. Horrified at the possibility of being deprived of what their stomachs had anticipated, the ringers began to argue with the rogues, but were insulted with the most rude and scandalous language. A fight broke out and the aggressors were driven out. The villains, however, had the audacity to creep in by a backdoor from Lady's Lane, but the ringers had anticipated their move and met them in the yard. At that moment, the second group of ringers arrived. A bloody fight took place which ended with the scoundrels being driven from the scene without a morsel of food!

According to J Armiger Trollope, a former Norwich ringer, in his book on the College Youths (1937), the Norwich Scholars always considered themselves to be as good as or better than any other company in England. Sometime before 1805 they issued a challenge to any twelve London ringers to ring for 100 guineas. The Norwich Company rang a peal of Oxford Treble Bob Royal in 5 hours 9 minutes. However, when the London ringers rang, they had to stop after 4000 changes when their tenor ringer collapsed, so the Norwich men won the match and the guineas.

Not everyone, however, appreciated Mancroft ringers. In May 1808 several residents raised a great outcry claiming their Sabbath rest was disturbed and demanded that Sunday ringing should be discontinued. Someone composed a verse:

> Ye rascals of ringers, ye terrible foes
> And disturbers of all who are fond of repose,
> How we wish for the quiet and peace of these lands
> That ye wore round your necks
> What ye pull with your hands.

The ringers took umbrage publishing a protest and demanded to know the name of the author. Later they concluded it was Joseph Miller, Esq.. The population of Norwich anticipated the bells would ring for national occasions. When this did not happen, there were complaints. In 1813 the Mayor decided not to pay for ringing Mancroft's bells on the occasion of the glorious victory by Wellington and his men in Spain. However, a party of gentlemen came forward and liberally subscribed a sum for similar purposes in the future.

When not in use the bells would normally be left with mouths down, so before ringing begins, all the bells have to be raised. The 1775 tenor required the strength of two or even three men together to raise it to the 'up' position. However, one man did have the muscle, for in 1806, after ringing for the funeral of Mr Richard Browne, baker, of St Martin's at Oak, it was remembered that he was the first man to raise the tenor at Mancroft single-handed.

Raising the Tenor

The medieval custom of ringing the tenor early in the morning and at 8 at night was still continuing in the nineteenth century. In 1810 the Sexton went to ring the 4am bell at Mancroft but to his great surprise, after pulling the rope – the sound produced was like 'an empty fish kettle'. He tried again but although the rope swung, there was silence. It was dark at that time of the morning and being without a light he could not ascend the belfry to ascertain the cause. Upon examination by daylight into the mystery, it appeared that the ball of the clapper was frozen against the side of the bell, a similar circumstance never having been known to happen before. The previous day there had been a heavy fall of snow accompanied by a high wind from the west. Snow had blown in through the louvres and frozen to the side of the bell. It remained stuck for several days.

Sometimes, after bells are raised ready for ringing, a clapper may finish resting on the wrong side of a bell (known as being 'up wrong'). When this happens it is often easier for someone to ascend the belfry and push it over. In 1811, James Vines, a ringer, then aged 78, attempted to turn the clappers of the two heaviest bells. He replaced the tenor clapper correctly then turned about on the frame to move the 11th when the tenor began to swing. He threw himself against the wheel but the edge of the bell caught him at the back of his legs. Fortunately, it was only a scratch. Had he been two inches nearer his legs would have been severed or he would have been precipitated into the bell and been crushed. He descended pale as a ghost but soon after joined in the ringing and after a cheerful glass with his companions later, he soon forgot the danger of the day.

When accidents happen the consequences can be disastrous. In 1814 the tenor broke just when the bells were ceasing. The bell had caught the frame knocking off a small piece of metal causing a crack in the bell 18 inches long and the width of a man's hand.

A new bell was ordered from Thomas Mears at the Whitechapel foundry, London, who gave its weight as 42cwt. By November 1814 the bell was ready for transportation by boat from London to Yarmouth. However, a delay was caused since none of the vessels had a hatchway wide enough to take it and were not willing to load it on the deck. Finally a captain agreed to the transportation if it could be taken out of the wagon and put on a truck till he could load it on his vessel. Unfortunately, the chain of the crane broke after it had raised the bell about six inches and it fell into the wagon. Thankfully

the bell was undamaged, but the captain refused to handle it again and it was returned to Whitechapel. The Custom House was approached and the bell was shipped on 3rd December 1814 to Yarmouth and then by wherry to Norwich. The cost of the bell, exclusive of carriage and hanging, was £110.

Before being hauled up the tower it was taken to the weighing machine in the Haymarket. Thomas Hurry, a young ringer in charge of the weighing, declared that the founder's weight was incorrect. This caused many arguments, but finally the new bell was 'opened' on 25th February 1815, just in time for the centenary of the first peal ever, rung at Mancroft in May 1715. Thirsty work; but beer was supplied by the churchwardens to Ansel, the bell hanger, John Trowse, who helped him, and the ringers. The new inscription read: 'TO KING QUEEN AND ROYAL FAMILY THIS HARMONIOUS PEAL IS DEDICATED / T. MEARS OF LONDON FECIT 1814', since by then, the royal children had increased beyond ten. The old tenor was broken up for easy transportation to London.

John Trowse was one of the few remaining ringers who had travelled to Lincolnshire in 1771 and Yorkshire in 1772. In 1804 he was in an attempted peal of Major on the back eight at Mancroft, with one man on the tenor. He was overpowered by the heat and had to stop. He was church sexton for 48 years and was landlord of the George Inn. He died in 1828 aged 83. Years later Douro Potter wrote:

'Once an old sexton of Mancroft could tell a good story, sing a good song, weave an excellent bit of fabric, splice a bell-rope, blow the tenor behind, but above all he could brew the most excellent ale and was landlord of the gabled old inn that stood by the parish pump on Hay Hill…Traditionally it owed its fine sparkling character to the crystal lymph used in the brewings drawn from the deep cool well by the parish pump. An employer in those days allowed his workmen beer so the churchwardens stood 16s worth of nut-brown ale to the ringers and carters who took the bell to be weighed. The Hayhouse where the weighing took place was near the George opening.'

(Years later the site of the old pump was discovered when the Haymarket was cleared for Sir Thomas Brown's statue.)

Mancroft employed two sextons, one for the church and one for the tower. In July 1821 Mr William Howes, who had been thirty-three years steeple sexton of St Peter Mancroft, died aged 85. Crowds gathered outside the tower to watch the funeral. His body was about to be interred in the churchyard near the tower doors by the Revd Mr Deeker, when the ceremony was interrupted by shouts and screams of the people watching. Two drunk drivers in charge of a gig and two horses came along Bethel Street, took the corner too quickly by the White Swan gates, were thrown out and narrowly missed being speared by the two iron spikes encircling the corner of the tower. Within days Jonathan Potter was chosen as steeple sexton of St Peter Mancroft without opposition. The Potter family were to have an influence on ringing at Mancroft for many years to come.

In April 1842, during the assizes, the company planned to ring a peal of 6729 changes of Stedman Cinques. However, after four and a half hours and about 6000 changes, the gudgeon of the tenor broke and the bell fell on the beams below with a tremendous crash; the ringers were apparently more frightened than hurt.

More work for the steeple sexton!

Ben Trent and Peter Sawyer, Steeple Keepers in 2014

St Peter Mancroft from the Haymarket c.1880

9
Samuel Thurston and his Era

Samuel Thurston, one of Norwich's most illustrious ringers, was born in the parish of St Martin at Oak, Norwich in 1789. He was elected a member of the Norwich Ringers' Benefit Society in 1803 at the tender age of fourteen, but was expelled in 1808 for ringing with a rival company. After paying a fine of 5s, he was reinstated. At twenty he had the confidence to perform at the New Theatre Public House on ten handbells tapping out various ringing methods from Bob Triples to Grandsire Caters. Since change ringing is based on permutations of numbers, this would have been a mathematical challenge. At the time his feat was considered the greatest performance ever completed by one person. He rang his first peal on tower bells later that year at St. Giles'. He married Mary Ann Coleman a year later in 1810 and they moved to St Martin at Palace. By then he was a self-employed master stonemason working at Norwich Cathedral from time to time, employing five or six workmen.

In 1813, rather full of self-importance, he challenged any man in England to a ringing competition for a £100 prize, to meet him at any twelve bell steeple not less than a hundred miles from Norwich, the winner to be judged on 'rapture'. He wanted Robert Chesnutt, the leader of the Mancroft Company, to join him and particularly wanted London men to participate. Chesnutt admonished Thurston through the local paper and strongly advised that if he wished to extricate himself from any more stupidity, he should propose a rational, proper, method of judging and declared that he would no further degrade himself by taking any notice of Thurston's foolish plans. Fortunately Robert Chesnutt, by his mild and persuasive manners, could restore friendship and promote reconciliation amongst the most contentious of men. (Robert Chesnutt and his brother John were hairdressers making wigs and tresses for performers at the Theatre Royal.) Thurston learned well from him, became a College Youth in 1813 and a member of Mancroft's band and the Norwich Scholars in 1814.

About 1814, the story goes he was pressed into the militia, much to his disgust, as he was a master stonemason and considered it a great degradation. One morning during drill, he was jamming gunpowder down his musket when he accidentally fired the powder and shot the ramrod into the air. Thereafter some of the ringers would refer to him as 'Sam, who fired away the ramrod.' Fond of relating stories, he used to amuse the ringers with his adventures. On one occasion, he had been ringing at Fakenham and after a drink or two with the ringers, was trudging home alone along a narrow lane when a greyhound came noiselessly alongside him and put its cold nose in his right hand. This startled him and he charged off only to trip over a sleeping donkey!

Thurston encouraged new recruits to Mancroft, always pushing them to achieve more. Sometimes, however, learners' efforts did not appeal to the general public. A correspondent observed that bells were not being rung in the style of excellence to which he was used and wondered if it was learners or the absence of skilled ringers. Practising finally paid off as in June 1815 eight of the Society of St Peter Mancroft rang a quarter peal – an intricate composition of Stedman Triples. Not be outdone, a rival band at St Michael's Coslany also rang a similar quarter in the same week.

On Monday, 8th February, the following year, a group of young ringers rang 1620 changes of Stedman Caters at Mancroft and on another occasion scored 1816 changes of Bob Royal, corresponding with the date of the year.

Later that year Helmingham, Suffolk, celebrated its new set of eight bells with a ringing competition to which thirteen teams entered and about 5000 people assembled in Helmingham Hall Park to listen. Ringing started at nine in the morning and continued most of the day. The Norwich ringers rang handbells at the Hall in the morning for the entertainment of the donor of the bells, the Right Honourable the Earl of Dysart. All the competition teams rang Bob Major, except the Norwich team who rang five different methods and impressed the listeners with their bold and regular striking. Afterwards the competitors were treated to food, port and sherry and given five shillings each. Two barrels of beer were provided for the crowd and a ball was held in the evening.

Thurston's house was full of clocks. He fitted some sort of contrivance into one of them, which when fully wound would repeat the words 'Don't fret', until it ran down. He was well known for his expertise and people would bring their clocks for repair. A notebook of his contains a list of the peals he rang in London and Norfolk and curiosities such a recipe for elderberry wine, how to make a spark of fire jump between a nose and a finger and instructions to make varnish for paper from turpentine, wine and milk.

Thurston's brilliance helped the Mancroft band to attain greater achievements. On 20th January 1817 they rang a peal of 5016 Norwich Court Bob Maximus in 4 hours and 2 minutes, claimed to be the first peal in the method in England:

Robert Chesnutt	Treble	George Hames	7th
Peckover Hill	2nd	John Trowse	8th
John Giddens	3rd	Joseph Lubbock	9th
Charles Gittings	4th	Thomas Hurry	10th
Samuel Havers	5th	Nathaniel Beales	11th
Charles Kelf	6th	Samuel Thurston	Tenor
		Matthew Smith	

Conducted by Robert Chesnutt

Thurston received a silver-gilt memento with the inscription: 'Presented to Mr Saml. Thurston, July 4th, 1825, by the united Ringers of St Peter Mancroft, for the eminent services in composing the peal of 5016 of Norwich Court twelve in, and ringing the tenor in a superior style.' It was last seen in a Norwich pawnshop in 1889. This presentation was made after Chesnutt had died, in 1821 aged 53, and when Thurston was the undisputed leader of the Mancroft ringers.

About the year 1819, Thurston took up bell hanging and hung the bells at Blofield and Worstead. It was reported in April 1825, the tenor at Mancroft, that formerly needed the strength of three men to ring, had been re-hung by Thurston and could be raised by one man using one hand. Thomas Hurry, also a ringer and bellhanger disputed this, saying that it was he who had repaired the bell four years ago and no one had attended to it since. In fact, after Hurry had rehung the tenor, Thurston was able to raise the bell with one hand 'by ingenuity known only to himself'!

One of Thurston's fellow ringers, George Watering, used the bells in a different way in 1820 ringing many tunes on the twelve at Mancroft, among them 'God Save The King', 'John of Paris', 'Oh dear what can the matter be' and 'Scots wha hae wi Wallace bled'.

Change ringing on handbells is performed with one bell in each hand. It was becoming popular in the early part of nineteenth century, perhaps because ringers could practise for hours without disturbing the public. Stedman on tower bells was considered difficult, but few ringers could manage it on handbells. In 1822, Thurston conducted a quarter peal of Stedman Triples on handbells, the first ever rung double-handed. He carved a stone tablet commemorating the event and the ringers

presented him with his portrait. The painting, about 15 inches by 10, showed him standing on the tenor box, a rope in one hand and a manuscript in the other. The tablet and a photograph of the painting can be seen in the ringing chamber. The portrait was last seen in St Michael's church, Macclesfield many years ago.

Hearing that the new church at Chelsea was to have a ring of 10 bells with the opening of them due in September 1823, the Mancroft ringers contemplated visiting London to do the opening with Thurston's composition of Stedman's principle and to use the opportunity to ring Stedman at London's 12-bell towers. There is no record of their visit; however, they did ring 3000 changes of Stedman Cinques at Mancroft shortly after that time.

A visit to Lavenham, Suffolk, in 1827 left them in financial difficulties to the extent of being obliged to sell or pawn their watches and part of their clothing in order to get home, where they arrived in a state of destitution! Unfortunately, no further details of this incident are known.

On 17th February 1827 the *Norfolk Chronicle* reported a peal of Oxford Treble Bob Royal, rung by the Mancroft Company at their home tower in 3 hours 52 minutes, conducted by Samuel Thurston and praised it as a masterpiece, particularly congratulating Thomas Hurry for ringing the tenor without assistance. In April, five of them rang 5120 changes of Oxford Treble Bob Major in 2 hours 20 minutes on handbells - described as 'an astonishing display of genius':

E. Mason 1, W. Mann 2, Henry Hubbard 3-4, James Hurry, 5-6, Joshua Hurry 7-8. Elijah Mason was the conductor.

A half peal of Stedman on handbells took place in April 1831, another triumph. The *Norwich Mercury* called it 'unparalleled' and 'astonishing' as each ringer rang two bells:

Samuel Thurston	1-2	Frederick Watering	5-6
Henry Hubbard	3-4	Joshua Hurry	7-8

Conducted by Samuel Thurston

In November they rang 6160 changes of Double Norwich Court Bob Major at St Michael's Coslany, conducted by Thurston, the longest length in that method and for years to come. In March 1832 they rang 6720 changes of Oxford Treble Bob Major, at St Giles, the first time this composition containing 120 course ends had been rung in Norwich.

Samuel Thurston 1822

38

Thurston was invited to London in 1829 to give advice on the famous Bow bells at St Mary-le-Bow church. His family joined him, but his wife thoroughly disliked the place and they returned to Norwich after about a year. This may be why the Norwich Scholars expelled him in May 1829, for 'improper conduct' - perhaps just ringing with another society as in 1808.

There were riots in England in 1831 when Parliament decided against changes to the electoral system which would have given towns and cities better representation. On the 15th October the news that the second Reform Bill had been defeated in the House of Lords reached Norwich. A few of those against reform tried to bribe the Mancroft ringers to raise the bells and ring a peal for this supposed triumph, but locals assembled round the church, preventing this and a possible riot.

Two of Thurston's most notable peals were rung on his return to Norwich. On 6th February 1835 he conducted a peal of Superlative Surprise Major at St Giles, only the second known peal in the method, the first having being rung at Huddersfield in 1821. On 17th November that same year he conducted a peal of London Surprise Major on the back eight bells at St Andrew's, the first ever peal in the method. What makes this peal even more remarkable is that ropes at St Andrew's fall in the order 1, 3, 2, 7, 10, 5, 4, 6, 9, 8. A peal board, recording both of these peals, hanging at St Giles records this as an 'insurmountable task'. It was also reported in the newspaper, stating:

'We had the pleasure of hearing from our scientific ringers 5,280 changes of that intricate composition London Surprise. This peal has been attempted by many of the most learned in the Science, but relinquished on account of its complexity, but in the hands of our Norwich ringers this obstacle soon vanished, and in 3 hours and 25 minutes a perfect peal was completed, thus showing what perseverance combined with industry and knowledge can attain.'

Norwich, St Andrew
17th November 1835 in 3 hours 25 minutes
5280 LONDON SURPRISE MAJOR

1 George Watering	5 James Truman
2 Elijah Mason	6 Robert Burrell
3 Frederick Watering	7 Charles Payne
4 Henry Hubbard	8 Samuel Thurston

Composed by William Shipway. Conducted by Samuel Thurston

In later years when Thurston was unable to ring tower bells, ringers would come to his house for instruction on handbells. He called them 'young stags'. When they rang on local tower bells, he would go to his bed chamber to listen using an ear horn and admonish them later for any mistakes.

On 9th January 1841, after dining at The Adam and Eve the night before, he collapsed and died aged 52. He was buried at the foot of Mancroft's tower. A memorial stone, to be seen today, subscribed for by 'the Exercisers at large', was erected nearby on the church wall.

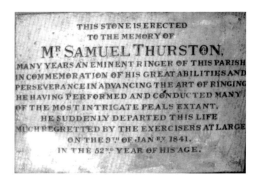

THIS STONE IS ERECTED
TO THE MEMORY OF
Mr SAMUEL THURSTON,
MANY YEARS AN EMINENT RINGER OF THIS PARISH
IN COMMEMORATION OF HIS GREAT ABILITIES AND
PERSEVERANCE IN ADVANCING THE ART OF RINGING
HE HAVING PERFORMED AND CONDUCTED MANY
OF THE MOST INTRICATE PEALS EXTANT,
HE SUDDENLY DEPARTED THIS LIFE
MUCH REGRETTED BY THE EXERCISERS AT LARGE
ON THE 9th OF JANry 1841,
IN THE 52nd YEAR OF HIS AGE.

The greatest respect was shown during his funeral. Shutters were closed, blinds were drawn and the bells of nearly every Norwich church were tolled. The following obituary was published:

'On Saturday, January 9th, died suddenly in the 52nd year of his age, Mr. Samuel Thurston, who was for more than 30 years one of St. Peter Mancroft ringers. As a practical ringer and theorist combined, the Art has lost one of its brightest ornaments, but though dead, the tablets erected in different parishes throughout the City and County will yet live to record his fame as a ringer, and those who best knew him can testify that the best ringers our City can boast of are indebted to this great artist in the profession for the knowledge they possess in the Art of Ringing, Norwich being able to compete with any other band of ringers.'

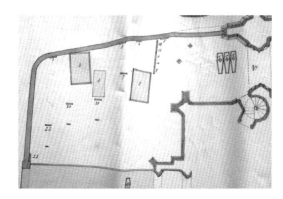

Samuel Thurston's grave is on the right of the three near the stairs going up the tower

Thomas Hurry and His Times

A good view of the White Swan with its yard could be seen from the top of Mancroft's tower. Occasionally barristers on circuit dined there. At the Norwich music festival of 1845 there were so many visitors that many inns were full. As much as 10s was paid at the inn for a couch for the night. Guests on New Year's Eve might well have listened for the sound of the bells before raising a glass to welcome in the New Year.

There were visitors in the ringing chamber in 1845. Standing in the centre was the thirty-two pint earthenware jug or gotch, lost for some years but lately recovered. A toast was proposed to the company and science of ringing, acknowledged by Thomas Hurry. Three times the bells were fired (all rung simultaneously) as a tribute to the royal family. Then Hurry rang the tenor to the admiration of the assembled company. The *Norfolk Chronicle* reported this event and there were other New Year celebrations while visitors watched the ringing. A mid-nineteenth century water colour of the ringing chamber by the artist Henry Ninham, on display in the transept, shows the jug in the centre of the room when the ringing chamber was about half way up the west window. The ringers, being nearer to the bells than today, would have found bell handling much easier, without the long draught of rope.

Thomas Hurry was one of the more controversial ringers of the time. Charles Payne, 'The Rambling Ringer' and close friend of Samuel Thurston wrote:

Then I went to Norwich where the dons do dwell,
Some of the ringers I knew very well.
There was Hurry, he railed against Thurston and Payne,
And swore he would never ring with them again.

Records suggest that Hurry was resourceful, generous, physically strong, energetic, self-important, both admired and disliked and of a masterful disposition. A skilful ringer, he joined the Ancient Society of College Youths in 1813 at the same time as Samuel Thurston. He was Feast Maker of the Benefit Society in 1821 when, unusually, the celebration took place over two days. The bill of fare included 7½ ounces of tobacco, 17 gallons of ale, 35½ pounds of beef, 18 pounds of veal and 17 pounds of mutton. On the first day the beef had to be roasted, a leg of mutton and knuckle of veal boiled with a breast of pork. On the second day a leg of veal was to be roasted with a leg and shoulder of mutton. Afterwards he presented the society with four pewter quart pots.

When the clapper of the eleventh bell broke in 1822 after the Norwich Scholars had rung 22 courses of Stedman Cinques, Hurry repaired it, claiming that its movement was so enhanced that a lad of 12 would be capable of ringing it.

Thomas Hurry came from a Ditchingham ringing family. He and his brother Joshua were regularly advertising as bellhangers from their base at the White Hart Inn, near Mancroft.

In 1822 the brothers rehung the six bells at St John Maddermarket in a new frame. They were opened on 10th October by the St Peter Mancroft Company with 720 changes of Treble Bob and 720 of Court Bob Minor. Several other peals and touches were rung during the day. The bells were judged to be the best ever of their weight. The Hurrys were praised for the mathematical exactness of their workmanship and the ringers declared they had never rung any bells whatsoever with so much ease.

Thomas Hurry was also steeple keeper at St Andrew's church in the city. The bell frame there was rather odd having started as a five bell frame set cornerwise in the tower with a frame above to make the five into an eight. When Hurry wanted to increase the bells to ten, he approached the church authorities. He thought he had their permission, ordered the bells and hung them in another frame above the eight. When he sent in his bill, the church denied all knowledge, so he was obliged to make a gift of them himself.

In 1826 the brothers fell out over the installation of new bells at Reedham after Joshua claimed to have done all the work.

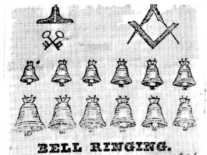

BELL RINGING.

On MONDAY, APRIL, 9th, *1826*

WILL be Opened, an entire NEW PEAL of FIVE BELLS at REEDHAM, Norfolk, which has been New Framed and New Hung by Mr. THOMAS HURRY, of this City, not Joshua Hurry as he stated to the Public in his advertisement in the Norfolk Chronicle dated Dec. 24, 1825. He assures them that the work was all done by his own hands and that his brother Joshua Hurry had no hand in the matter Mr. Thomas Hurry can prove by many Clergymen, and near 60 Gentlemen who happened to be Churchwardens during the last eight years, that the said Joshua Hurry never had been employed by any person whatever in the Bell Business only by his brother Thomas Hurry, who always treated him as one of the family, and paid him handsomely for what work he ever did.

At the Opening of the Reedham New Bells there will be given THREE PRIZES to those Companies of Change Ringers who happen to Ring the best Peals or 720 Changes, as will be agreed on the morning of opening the bells.

Good Accommodation at Mr. Goffen's and Mr. Sheppard's, the only two Public Houses in the town.

Advertisement, 1826, by Thomas Hurry after the brothers fell out.

In 1827, when Thomas Hurry was headsman of the benefit society, the Purse, he became the first person to ring Mancroft's tenor, weighing 41cwt, single-handed, to a peal lasting for nearly four hours. It was described as a masterly performance.

A board commemorating this peal is in the style of the three earliest peal boards, except it is larger, to allow for a piece about Hurry and it has a crown above instead of a bell. In the past, several ringers had tried to accomplish this feat without success. It seems that Hurry fully intended to keep his record. A few years later, a man called Smith (no further details are known of him) wanted to ring the tenor single-handed to a peal. Hurry was needed, so they pretended that they going for long 'touch'. All went well for a time and the end seemed in sight, but then Hurry realized what they were up to, set his bell, and, turning to the tenor man, said: 'Never as long as I live!'

The posts of church sexton and tower sexton were advertised after the death of John Trowse in 1828. Thomas Hurry applied, insisting that he was the best candidate as he had been brought up amongst bells, a ringer for forty years and fifteen of those at St Peter Mancroft with care of the bells for the last eight. He was not successful and a month later the ringers were reported to have celebrated 'with much conviviality' at the Pope's Head Inn the appointment of Jonathan Potter as church sexton and John Thompson as steeple sexton. Some years later, George Potter inherited the post from his father.

George Potter was responsible for supervising grave digging. In 1840 workmen were digging a vault for the body of Mrs Bowman, wife of the vicar. Accidentally, they broke through a coffin containing the remains of Sir Thomas Brown (physician, philosopher and author), who had been buried in Mancroft in 1682. Mr Fitch, a local antiquary, was sent for and the skull and some of the auburn hair were removed. Dr E Lubbock, who made a collection of artifacts of this kind, apparently purchased them for his collection, where they remained until 1845 when they were handed over to the museum of the Norfolk and Norwich Hospital. The skull was finally returned to the church and reburied in 1922. A descendent of George Potter was very unhappy that his grandfather could be accused of the skull theft. He wrote a poem that was published in the parish magazine and subsequently quoted in *The Bellringer* on 1st May 1907:

Who Stole The Skull?
Herbert E Potter

In this old Church, this ancient pile,
My fathers many years have served,
Their feet have trod each footworn aisle,
Nor paced its gloomy vaults unnerved.
Oft have I heard my father talk
Of heaps of skulls and stacks of bones,
Grim skeletons as white as chalk
That lay in their sepulchral tombs.
How once at noon, his father found
A body snatcher at a grave;
And stealthily without a sound,
He laid his hands upon the knave.
But as the robber begged, in tears,
His captor for his liberty,
He bade him drive away his fears
And with a caution set him free.
Of how a sexton, long ago,
Worked at his bench one Sunday night
Within the vaults, helped by the glow
That flickered from a candle light;
And bending o'er a piece of stone,
The candle singed his hoary hair;
And at the sound, without a groan,
He fainted there and then with fear.
Of how a ringer used to boast
That he of darkness had no dread;

And of all places he loved most
Was down the vaults among the dead.
And how he took the key one night
To go and ring the curfew bell.
He scorned the thought to take a light,
He knew the ins and outs too well.
But as it happened that same day,
The diggers of a grave, in haste,
To pack their tools and get away,
Forgot to put the slab in place.
And down the hole the ringer fell,
And midst the coffins stunned he lay
Until he woke, when, with a yell,
He very soon made haste away.
And nevermore he went, I'm told,
Into the Church without a light.
Alas how very brave and bold
We all are till we've had a fright.
And other tales I recollect,
Unmixed with tones of bravery,
But ne'er a word that could connect
His father's name with knavery,
So those are very wrong who say,
And in writing put it down,
That my grandfather stole away
The skull of great Sir Thomas Browne.

Samuel Thurston's sudden death in 1841 must have been a severe blow to the Norwich ringers. At Mancroft, the new ringing master was James Truman, an excellent ringer, but he did not have the charisma of Thurston. Other experienced ringers included Henry Hubbard, peal ringer, conductor and composer and Charles Middleton, famed for his composition of Cambridge Surprise Major.

During 1842 the church was closed for over a week, since it had not been thoroughly cleaned for twelve years. An article in the *Eastern Daily Press* in 1968 by Jonathan Mardle, describes Mancroft about the year 1840: 'The interior, at that time, was furnished with high dark box pews. Benches for the poor stood on either side of a broad path between the pews… There were no evening services because there were no lights. On Christmas afternoon candles were placed along the edges of the pews and boughs of holly were stuck in holes in the woodwork…The vicar, or upper minister was a short handsome old man with a cork leg. He wore knee breeches… Two beadles in dark braided gowns marched about the church carrying wands and then stood like statues. There were women pew-openers, to open the doors of the pews for those who had rented them.'

A board records a notable peal of Stedman which included Hurry, Truman, Hubbard and Middleton:

On Thursday January 18th 1844 Was rung in this Steeple that most intricate and ingenious Peal called Stedman's Cinques in Five hours and Seventeen minutes, consisting of 7126 Changes, without the misplacing of a bell or the repetition of a single change. The bold and regular striking attracted the notice of the Public, and is allowed to exceed any other performance ever attempted in England upon Twelve bells. The Peal was conducted by JAMES TRUMAN and rung by the under-mentioned persons. The Ministers and Churchwardens with a portion of the Inhabitants have contributed to the erection of this Tablet, the remainder being subscribed by the Company of Ringers.

THOMAS HURRY	TREBLE	WILL^M FREEMAN	7th
ROB^T BURRELL	2nd	GEO^R WATERING	8th
ELIJAH MASON	3rd	JAMES TRUMAN	9th
CHA^S MIDDLETON	4th	JOSHUA HURRY	10th
WILLIAM GAUL	5th	HENRY HUBBARD	11th
JOHN GREENWOOD	6th	GEORGE SMITH ⎱	TENOR
		ROB^T PALGRAVE ⎰	

MR BENJ^M CUNDALL. MR JOHN EASTO. CHURCHWARDENS

Trollope writing in 1925 knew Palgrave and Freeman who remembered the excellent striking.

By this time the Hurry brothers had become reconciled and were advertising from The White Horse Inn on Hay Hill adjoining to St Peter Mancroft.

George Potter, sexton, sided with two thirds of the ringers during a rift with Thomas Hurry in 1845. Acrimonious correspondence in the *Chronicle* began early in 1845 when a notice was printed asking all correspondence to the St. Peter's Society of Ringers to be sent to the Black Prince Tavern in the Market Place since Thomas Hurry was no longer a member.

1st March (Hurry): 'He was the leader of the society and all letters should be sent to him at Lady's Lane.'

8th March (Ringers including George Potter and Joshua Hurry): 'It was 'positively untrue that Hurry was the leader "we know of no leader but the conductor" and "Hurry's turbulence and miss-rule" had lost some good ringers.'

15th March (Hurry): 'The Benefit Society 'St Peter Mancroft Society of Ringers' was dissolved and then re-established with the same name and he was a member of the old society. The Benefit Society was not the same as the company of ringers.'

22nd March (Ringers front page): 'Our old friend Hurry has to our great surprise, admitted the truth, that he is not a member…all communications should be addressed to the Sexton…' Hurry resigned.

Just nine months on Thomas Hurry was clearly in charge with no evidence over what brought the change. His skills were probably needed since the band would have sorely missed the expertise of Samuel Thurston. The Benefit Society re-formed in March 1846 with Thomas Hurry and Thomas Burrell as the first supervisors. Rules included no fighting, no drinking to excess; none to have a venereal disease. Meetings were to be held at the Black Prince Tavern.

Thomas Burrell. He was Supervisor with Thomas Hurry in 1846.
Died 21ˢᵗ November 1875 aged 80.
Sexton of St George Colegate 58 years and 56 years a ringer at St Peter Mancroft.

Shortly after these disputes improvements were made to the churchyard by lowering the earth banks around the church. No one could have failed to see the quantity of human bones piled against the outer wall to the level of the window at the south-west corner. They had been found in a charnel house under the church and after a heavy fall of rain the mass of skulls and bones was exposed. A deep pit was quickly dug and the bones re-interred.

Ringing in the New Year at Mancroft, a watercolour by Henry Ninham, mid-nineteenth century
(Reproduced with permission of St Peter Mancroft Church)

As time went on Hurry found ringing more difficult. Henry Daines in 1924 remembered that he was of big, heavy build and, when very old and broken, used to ring the second at Mancroft half sitting on a high chair. From 1851 Hurry was receiving sickness payments from the Benefit Society and spent his last few years as an out-pensioner of the Great Hospital. He died aged 86 in 1869 and was buried at Ditchingham.

His portrait shows him with a handbell in each hand, a glass of wine on the table and a drawing of St Peter Mancroft's tower on the wall, or perhaps a view from a window.

Thomas Hurry (Norfolk Record Office, SO 78/34 733x2)

11

Tower Scenes

By the mid-nineteenth century the churchyard was piled high with burials: paths through ran between tall brick walls, up to six feet high on the north side. There was no path under the tower since the arches were filled to form a space for the parish fire engine, hoses and fire buckets.

St Peter Mancroft showing the blocked-up space under the tower after the restoration

From the White Swan Inn the 'Magnet' coach to London left at seven in the evening and returned at seven in the morning. Apparently the splendid animals and skillful driver were out of the yard at the first stroke of seven from the big bell at Mancroft and before the clock had finished striking the team and coach were well round St Stephen's corner.

The door from the church to the stairway leading to the ringing chamber and beyond is carved with the Latin words:

1847 Georgius Potter Sacristanus Dono dedit,

Translated roughly: George Potter, sacristan, the donor. George Potter joined the Purse Club in 1848. He would regularly entertain the ringers at the White Hart, near the church, with practice bouts against Ned Painter a bare-knuckle prize fighter, whose nickname was 'Fisticuff'.

He championed the ringers, making sure that they received just payment for their services. In 1866 he complained on one occasion that they were only offered six and a half guineas for ringing for a civic occasion when they were entitled to eight. When Potter warned the ringers to meet at a certain time to ring for a job, he expected them to be prompt. They were fined three pence for being a fraction late, sixpence for within quarter of an hour and one shilling and six pence for not coming at all. When Alfred James Rush, the Stanfield Hall murderer, was condemned to death in 1848, Potter was one of his watchers at Norwich Castle and played crib with him. After the execution the cap Rush had worn was given to Potter by the hangman as a memento.

St Peter Mancroft with the White Horse on the right

Most years the citizens of Norwich had heard the bells more frequently from Advent to Christmas. It was known as the 'Ringing Season': 'The first exciting peal apparently thrilled the young with anticipation, and reawaked the happy memories of the past for the elderly. During the New Year celebrations in 1864, the market place was thronged with people and inside the tower the ringing chamber was decked with holly and evergreens. The churchwardens and several ladies and gentlemen ascended the tower and spent half an hour with the ringers. The health of the ringers was drunk from the jug filled with steaming liquor and a new chandelier, purchased by the churchwardens and manufactured by Mr E W Potter, was presented. Thanks were expressed for the decorative embellishments of the sexton. On New Year's Eve 1866 George Potter had

51

carpeted the floor with evergreens, decorated the walls and ceiling, and hung Chinese lanterns.

That year the organ was removed from the west gallery. The ringers could then be seen by the congregation for the first time, revealing that ringing took some physical effort. The congregation expressed disapproval! On 14th December 1867 the *Norwich Mercury* reported that the ringers assembled on a Sunday evening:

'and to their utter astonishment and mortification they found the belfry locked against them; upon enquiring the reason they were told - will it be scarcely be credited - that the act of ringing involved 'manual labour'...Facts should be known that St Peter's bells - acknowledged the grandest peal in England - are regarded somewhat in the light of public property having been publicly subscribed for by the Corporation and the leading inhabitants of both county and city...Alas! For the moment it stands threatened by an act of 'official' caprice, an arbitrary, unprecedented exercise of brief authority - disapproved of, it is understood, by the respected minister...'

The correspondent expressed the hope that 'the glorious old St Peter's bells' would be heard the next Sunday evening, and in the future.

Both George Potter and Thomas Hurry died in 1869, losses felt keenly by the ringers especially as they were about to enter a problematical period. George was succeeded by his son Douro Thomas as church sexton with the privilege of occupying the Peter room over the north porch and the name 'Peter' when on duty. As a lad Douro went to America with an elder brother, a stonemason in New York, and stayed for several years. After his return, high up in a buttress of the tower, he carved a figure of St Barbara in a niche. In the crown of the canopy he cut a hole, later embedded in masonry, where he hid a small role of parchment with the dates of Jonathan and George and the words: 'all the stones in this section of the buttress including the niche and canopy were wrought and fixed by me Douro Thomas Potter, sexton since 1868. I was taught to use the mallet and chisel in New York.' An article written in the 1890s recorded that the figure of St Peter in a window in the church (by then removed) reminded the writer of Potter the sexton in his official gown, with a straw hat (the halo) on the back of his head and the keys of the church in his hand.

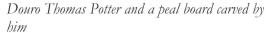

Douro Thomas Potter and a peal board carved by him

Sextons of Mancroft were responsible for church decorations during church festivals, and these could be quite elaborate at Christmas. While ringers were in the tower in 1872, the citizens of Norwich were having a different experience outside in the market area. The *Norwich Mercury* gave the following account:

NEW YEARS EVE

The old Norwich custom of the citizens gathering in the marketplace to greet the New Year seemed on Tuesday night to be a strictly observed as ever.

Notwithstanding that rain fell fast when the old year had nearly passed away, the market place was crowded by thousands of people. Probably it was the announcement that the bands of Edmond's and Day's menageries could also be present that was sufficient to entice the citizens to leave their homes at such an hour…They were, however, greatly deceived, for so admirably did the bands strive to drown each other's strains, that only the greatest discordance and inharmony, was to be heard. First Edmond's band were drawn in their van by team of dromedaries from the castle Hill to the marketplace, on entering which they commenced playing the appropriate air of 'Auld Lang Syne'. The congregated citizens were fated not long to enjoy the really excellent playing of this band for in a short time there entered into the marketplace another van, drawn by a team of dromedaries, but with the addition of an elephant. … Above the horrid din which they were so successful in making, was to be heard the lusty feverish beat of drum, and the playing of a cracked trombone by a frantic fellow who seemed to be glorying in the torture he was inflicting upon the assembled people…These having

53

taken up their places at the further into the marketplace, the strain of yet another band of music was heard proceeding from the same quarter…But at last their strains died away, the beat of the drum only surviving, and the solo that followed the ungrateful mob did not appreciate. Fain would the crowd have clapped their hands to their ears, and shut out the discord thus created, but that the rain still fell and the umbrellas must be kept up. A few minutes to twelve, first one and then the other bands had succumbed and then Edmund's band snatched this interval of quietude to play "Hale smiling morn"…Twelve o'clock struck, the bells of St Peters fired, another year had come upon us and congratulations were exchanged. This blessed state, however, was not long to remain for the van which was stationed at the other end of the Market envying the other's audience, advanced and drove quite close up and again commenced puffing out their horrid noise; exciting the wrath of the crowd. Another interval of quiet and then the "Hallelujah chorus" was played in the excellent manner in which Edmund's band is famed. The Market Place was soon after reduced to its wonted quietness, the heavy rain driving indoors all who had any love of comfort. The conduct of the people was for the most part orderly. A few, however, wearing the uniform of a certain corps conducted themselves in everything but an orderly manner – 'the festivities of the season' having fairly overcome them.

Bosworth Harcourt captured the spirit of New Year celebrations in the ringing chamber in 1872

A visitor to the tower in 1874 described his experience in an article in the ringers' journal, *The Bell News*:

'It was a lovely summers evening when I looked up the conductor of the Norwich band – a veteran ringer, who rang his first peal nearly 50 years ago. With him I ascended the massive tower… We then proceeded up to the present ringing chamber, lighted by the upper portion of a grand west window, through which the sun was streaming…The eight back bells were then raised in peal in excellent style. This is a branch of ringing which London ringers, perhaps unwisely, neglect; for the tone of the bell is never so sweet and pure as when they are about three parts up. We next ascended to the bells and saw the tenor erect in the centre of the tower surrounded by her melodious sisters.'

Work in progress on St Peter Mancroft's tower c.1880
(Image courtesy of Norfolk County Council Library and Information Service)

The tower was showing wear and tear. Stones were splitting away from the walls after frost. A survey in 1878 declared that the facing on some buttresses was positively unsafe and fund-raising began. The body of the church reopened in 1881 at the end of a stage in restoration which had been moving westward in fits and starts during the previous forty years or so; but the tower required much work still to be done and the bells could only be chimed. In 1882 the graveyard was leveled, gravestones removed and earth and bones carted away to the public cemetery. Burials ceased thereafter and the sexton became the verger. The way under the tower was opened at the same time. After the fire appliances had been removed, the space was let out to traders for many years.

At a meeting in Norwich of the Norwich Diocesan Association of Ringers (founded 1877), the vicar of Swaffham, gave an address to 200 members in 1879. He began:

'If bells had the tongues of men instead of clappers…could they reveal the profanity and unseemly jesting eye, and drinking in the belfries - that while they gave out their hallowed music, which floated over hill and dale, unhallowed mirth was indulged in by the ringers.' He concluded that all that was about the old ringers and the new generation of ringers were 'privileged to live in an age when the Church had awakened from its sleep'.

Times were changing and the ringers' jug would soon be a matter of controversy.

12
Ringing Changes

The restoration of the tower with the addition of turrets and fleche, was a massive undertaking and the bells were silent between 1881 and 1883. During this period the bells were rehung by Messrs. George Day and Son of Eye, Suffolk. The ringing chamber was moved to a position lower down in the tower, new clappers, stock and wheels were provided for the bells and iron guides with polished wooden bosses for the ropes to pass through, since the ringers would have to cope with an additional twenty feet (6 metres) of rope. Meanwhile the ringers rang at other towers. In September 1883, when Frederick Knights was Ringing Master, they took the Great Eastern Railway to London to meet members of the College Youths. In the morning they rang at Spitalfields, Whitechapel and St Saviour's in Southwark and took a tour of St Paul's Cathedral. Lunch was enjoyed at the King's Head, Winchester Street, followed by a trip by steam boat to Rochester Row. During afternoon tea it was discovered that a member of their party, known as Poor Peter, was missing. Fortunately, the Steeple Keeper had heard where they were heading and returned him to the party. After tea they rang at Bow, and St Michael's Cornhill. Handbells were rung at the King's Head, Winchester Street, headquarters of the College Youths.

Over a hundred visitors attended the reopening of the bells in April 1883, followed by a substantial celebratory dinner at the White Hart. Gervas Holmes Esq., partner in the Redenhall Bell Foundry, proposed a toast and expressed the hope that the magnificent bells would encourage Mancroft ringers once again to take the lead in the country as they had done forty or fifty years ago. Two attempts at ringing a peal failed, but on the 5th November 1883 a peal of 5080 Kent Treble Bob Royal was rung at Mancroft in 3 hours 35 minutes, the longest length rung on the bells with one man on the tenor.

The St Peter Mancroft Society, Norwich Scholars, was re-established in 1883.

A certificate of the Society of Norwich Scholars 1884.
The original hangs in Tasburgh tower.

Monday 5th November 1883, prior to the peal of Kent Treble Bob Royal, with the bell they rang:

Top row Left to Right: John Fiddament (5), Philip Sadler (2), James Skinner (8), Nathaniel J Pitstow (Treble and conductor), Rev N Bolingbroke, Captain Moore, James Youngs, William Smith (9)
Seated 2nd row: George Smith (Tenor), William Freeman, Charles Middleton, Robert Palgrave, Frederick Knights (7)
Bottom row: William Blyth, Henry Roberts, Douro Thomas Potter senr., Edward Freeman jr.

William Ireland (3), Frederick Pitstow (4) and Robert Stackwood (6), are not in the photograph.

Charles Middleton died in a Norwich workhouse in September 1886, aged 73. He was born at Marsham, a village near Aylsham, moved to Norwich in 1839 and was elected to the St Peter Mancroft Company in 1843. Middleton is famously remembered for his peal composition of Cambridge Surprise Major.

In January 1888, after ringing at the church, members of the St Peter's Society and about one hundred and fifty ringers from surrounding villages, adjourned to the White Hart to open new handbells with a course of Grandsire Cinques. The evening concluded with tune ringing accompanied by Philip Sadler on the piano.

An outing to West Norfolk in June 1889 took them by train to Swaffham where they noted two early peal boards of Bob Major and Garthon's Triples, both dated 1740. They soon discovered a scarcity of sign posts in that part of Norfolk. At Oxborough, ringing was interrupted by 'imperious interference by the local schoolmistress' and so they left in disgust.

The White Hart, St Peter's Street

Later that year Arthur Hubbard, a visitor, came to join them for a peal at Mancroft. Ringing began at 3.18pm and soon settled down to a comfortable rhythm. By 6 o'clock, the light was beginning to fade and the conductor began to worry. Ten minutes later, he realized that there were 1000 changes to go and the speed of ringing increased with anxiety. During the last 500 changes, the ropes were nearly invisible. A feeling of relief all round when the last single was called and then the words: 'That's All' and Holt's ten part peal of Grandsire Triples had been scored.

In June 1894 the ringers took the train to London's Liverpool Street Station, where they were 'welcomed by a 'mixture of smoke, fog and dirt from falling brickwork…occasioned by alterations at present going on at that terminus.' Members of the College Youths piloted them about to St Sepulchre Snow Hill, St Margaret's Westminster, St Mary's Lambeth, St Barnabas' Pimlico, St Clement Danes and St Michael Cornhill. A few stayed on for another day to ring at St Paul's Cathedral where 'The hair of the four of us who rang there has only just regained its normal position after having stood upright at the sound of this glorious peal.' At the Imperial Institute, Kensington, two furnaces in the ringing chamber were full of boiling tar for the purpose of asphalting the floor. No health and safety worries in those days!

Frederick Knight's marriage was celebrated in 1892, with a peal of Kent Treble Bob Major on the eight back bells and recorded elaborately in the peal book.

Charles Borrett, a young man of some means, entertained the Mancroft ringers to a seven course dinner at the Central Restaurant in 1896 in celebration of his twenty-first birthday. An outing to Yarmouth by train the same year was enjoyed by all and parcels of bloaters were brought back for the married ones 'missuses'. Later that year a peal of Oxford Treble Bob Royal was rung at Mancroft in three hours forty-four minutes, the first peal of Royal by a local band for more than 68 years.

In 1900 the local historian Walter Rye gave the scroll containing the Articles of the Purse to the church; he had discovered it in Exeter.

The Revd Frederick Meyrick was appointed to Mancroft in 1901 and fell out with the ringers almost immediately. A parish magazine for February 1903 reported:

'The relation of the Mancroft bell ringers to the church is hardly satisfactory, and the vicar has told them so…Meanwhile it is not to the ringers, but to the chimers, to whom we are Sunday by Sunday indebted. The ringers only ring on Festivals and in Advent. A Guild of Chimers, under the Superintendence of Mr Potter has been formed, and we welcome them as real voluntary workers in the church's cause…'

The vicar wanted the ringers to be part of the congregation and give their skills freely and accused them of using the bells as a means of making money. Charles Borrett, on behalf of the ringers, explained the effort needed to ring for services as the bells were heavy and ringers had to be in the tower for an hour before the service.

Much of the contention focused around the ringers' jug. During the church restoration it had been given to Douro Potter, both ringer and sexton for safe custody. Potter died in 1893 and it was then lodged in the sacristy and thereby the ringers were deprived of possession of what was theirs. To the ringers the jug was a symbol of their proud history and part of the traditional New Year's Eve celebrations. To the vicar, it encouraged the use of alcohol in the church and he refused to return it to the ringing chamber. He wrote 'no doubt the wicked, but grateful and comforting 'hot-pot', a generous compound of ale and spirits, went round merrily enough in Dersley's time – but we live in a pernickety age'. In 1906 the Benefit Society members decided to hold a concert in their club room to celebrate £100 being held in the fund and asked the vicar to release the jug for that one occasion. He declined and a request for a reconsideration led to three ringers appearing before the Church Council. Subsequently, a churchwarden's terse letter was received by Frederick Knights: 'Sir - After careful consideration of the minute book, the rules of the company and the relation of the ringers to the church, we regretfully feel that it is our duty to close the belfry for ringing purposes.'

Members of the congregation asked for an explanation. The vicar wrote in the church magazine that after vain efforts to put things on a satisfactory basis, the churchwardens and he felt they had to close the belfry and start again with a new company. 'Soon he hoped the beautiful bells would ring again, and that the ringers would take an honoured place among the Church-workers of the parish.'

Mancroft Ringing Chamber 1895

Treble, Alfred Brighton, 2. ?, 3. Edward Ward, 4. Albert Warnes, 5. James Skinner, 6. George Howchin, 7. ? 8. ? 9. ?, 10. Fred Howchin, 11. George Smith, Tenor Fred Knights senior

13
Out with the Old. In with the New.

'The majestic edifice of St Peter Mancroft church stood out in dark relief, but the deep toned voices of the bells were silent…' so reported a local newspaper. Over a hundred people had gathered in the Market Place at midnight 1907, hoping to celebrate to the sound of the bells; but the ringers had been locked out of the tower.

Reported comments included:

'It looks very much like trying to kick the old birds out of the nest.'

'The ringers call themselves Corporation ringers and look upon themselves as a body more or less independent of the church.'

'The sooner the authorities at St Peter Mancroft church set themselves seriously to the task of getting together and training a new company of ringers the better.'

Bosworth Harcourt, the amateur artist who recorded the New Year celebrations in the tower in 1872, wrote verses that appeared in the *Eastern Daily Press* 2nd January 1907. An extract:

Mancroft Bells
And they are silent, those tuneful iron tongues,
Those clanging monitors of "peace on earth",
Those twelve grand soothers of so many wrongs,
Those glorious tellers of a Saviour's birth.

For more of years than those who live can tell
Those bells of Mancroft have in Advent days
Warm'd the cold heart, and made the bosom swell
With gratitude, and tuned the lips to Praise.

But new men come and new ideas arise;
They deem *their* voices, when the great Day's a'dawn,
Are loftier than the Bells, to reach the skies,
And preach to men of the great Saviour born.

- They may be right. Who knows? Only my conscience tells
At Christmastide I'd rather hear "The Bells".

Frederick Knights wrote to the press defending the ringers. He explained that he and the others would have been willing to ring for services, but had never been approached. He felt that any fair-minded person would agree that men having home ties and families and living in all parts of the city, would find it almost impossible to attend all the services, especially since ringers had to be in the tower nearly an hour before worship commenced and again afterwards. Most of the ringers were working men and some attended their own parish church.

It was a period when drunkenness was a problem. Encouraged by the Bishop, a temperance group was started at Mancroft. No wonder the ringers' reputation for enjoying a pint after leaving the belfry and actually imbibing from the famous ringers' jug in the ringing chamber on New Year's Eve was looked upon with horror. The vicar complained that 'the ringers were entirely out of touch with the church's life.' The ringers complained that their jug was locked in the sacristy. How times had changed! A century before, the ringers were often paid in porter and beer.

Daniel Holme, a member of the congregation, suggested the vicar should establish a new society. A meeting on 7th February 1907 was chaired by the vicar supported by the churchwardens. Those from the old company, who attended church services (not necessarily at Mancroft) and were prepared to ring without payment, were invited to join. Among them were Douro Thomas Potter, the verger, son of Douro, Egbert, Harry and Charles E Borrett, George P Burton and John E Burton. These formed the core of the new St Peter Mancroft Guild of Ringers, a title that continues today. The first practice took place on 19th February 1907; service ringing started in May and continued on Sundays thereafter. The vicar was most encouraging, providing the bells were not rung for political purposes. Members of the congregation were invited to view the ringing and encouraged to learn. The belfry was improved by panelling, (formerly old pew doors), red felt mats for the stone seats and a hand basin.

The new society, largely composed of learners, could not be expected to do justice to a heavy ring of 12 with long draughts of rope. Alexander (Alec) Potter, brother of Douro Thomas, was a new recruit, who aged sixteen, rang his first peal in 1907. However, the abilities of the new society were very inferior to the old band - and the public noticed!

The *Eastern Daily Press* reported a complaint in January 1907:

'Sir - if the sample of bell-ringing to which we were treated last night might be taken as indicative of the probable efforts of a new company, it is obvious to all who reside within hearing of the bells, are much interested in getting this 'storm-in-a-jug' patched up as soon as possible…One would have liked to fill the ringers' jug and pour the contents down the throats of, or over, the novices whose unrhythmical attempts were so persistently distracting…the art should not be acquired at the expense of annoying others.'

Ringing by gas light could not have been easy and the old gas pipes were leaking. George Burton, elected as the first Ringing Master, sensibly decided that 8 bells should be rung for services manned by ringers in rotation. Most ringing was done on the middle eight bells with 9th as tenor - an imperfect octave. Efforts by the ringers to raise money for a new flat 6th bell to form a true light octave began in 1908. The cost was raised by 1910, the new bell was cast by Messrs. Mears and Stainbank of Whitechapel, hung in a steel frame and named 'Gabriel'.

What of the old ringers? They continued to maintain the Benefit Society, ring handbells and practise at other towers in the city. They met socially in a club room at the Walnut Tree Shades. Charles Borrett had been taught by them and never lost touch. Old Fred Knights always offered him a cigar as soon as he sat down. Alfred Brighton, taught by Fred, rang his first peal of Stedman Cinques at Ipswich, cycling from Norwich and back on a penny farthing bicycle. Edward Francis, of 'genial manner and high spirits', composer of plain methods, died in 1911. The old ringers were invited to join with the new band to ring a muffled peal in his memory at Mancroft.

The Guild maintained a closer connection with the congregation. In 1912, the church celebrated its history with a colourful pageant produced by Nugent Monck involving several ringers. Charles Borrett took the part of Sir Peter Reade - very appropriate since Sir Peter had given 11 tenements to the Corporation in 1568 so the great bell of St Peter Mancroft might be rung at 4am and 8pm daily for the benefit of travelers, a custom that had lapsed by that date.

After a long length of major on handbells:
Left to right: Charles E Borrett, George P Burton, J Armiger Trollope, John E Burton

Norwich, St Peter Mancroft
The Parish Rooms
Thursday 26th April 1894, in 5 hours 10 minutes
11,200 Plain Bob Major
1-2 J Armiger Trollope   5-6 John E Burton
3-4 George P Burton   7-8 Charles E Borrett
Composed by J Armiger Trollope. Conducted by Charles E Borrett
This is the longest peal ever rung on handbells in any method,
and the longest length in Norwich for 157 years.

14
Bells and Belles

Up until the First World War the bells of St Peter Mancroft had only been rung by men; but this was about to change. Several of the ringers were in the forces including the Ringing Master. Most of the ringers were absent at some time during the period. These included: Frank H Phillips, Henry Borrett, Walter Cutbush, John Lemmon, C Thaine, Frederick Cross, William Hempel, Charles Gymer, Benjamin Thompson, Walter Rix, William Mayers and Alec Potter. John Burton was fit for 'sedentary' work only. The Mancroft Guild of Ringers suffered a consequent loss of numbers and invited a 'limited number of ladies' to join in 1916 as probationers. John Burton taught Miss George (Christian name unknown) and they married in 1922.

Benjamin Thompson suffered gas poisoning and was never able to ring much after the war. Alec Potter, son of the sexton Douro T Potter enlisted with the 8th Norfolks and was promoted to sergeant in 1915. He was wounded in France that year; buried alive, but survived after four months in hospital. In 1918 he was back in hospital with severe gunshot wounds. Walter Rix initially joined the Hunts Cyclist Battalion and later transferred to the Warwickshire Regiment. He was reported missing in 1915 and sadly never returned. William Hempel joined the Australian Infantry and was killed on 4th October 1917. He is commemorated on the Menin Gate at Ypres. The bells were not heard at 5.30am on Christmas Day morning due to lighting restrictions.

Sergeant Alec Potter

Private Walter Ernest Rix

The ladies, Miss Frances Bill, Miss Helen W Bill, Miss Hilda Durrant, Miss May Durrant and Miss D Seymoure were elected to full membership in 1917. Maintaining Sunday ringing was still a struggle, but continued thanks to the ladies.

Bells rang out over the city in thanksgiving at the end of the war. The first practice after Armistice Day took place in May 1919 when there were more ringers than ropes. Mancroft ringers declared that their lady ringers were capable of taking part in a touch on twelve bells, unlike many towers around the country. A request, in 1921, for more time to practise, was agreed. That year May Durrant rang a peal of Bob Royal, the first lady to do so for the Norwich and Ipswich Association. A joyful peal was rung for her marriage to Francis McHugh in June 1922 at Mancroft, with Douro Potter taking over the ringing of the tenor the last 35 minutes. The same year John Burton married Miss George, who joined in 1921. However, by 1924, they were struggling for ringers. At the time Mancroft was the only tower in Norwich where bells were rung regularly.

Douro Thomas Potter, ringer, verger and steeple keeper was adjusting a rope in the belfry early in 1924 when he noticed that the frame of the bell was rotting. He mentioned the fact to Mrs Agnes M Clark, daughter of Mr A. R. Chamberlin, a former churchwarden at Mancroft. She agreed to pay for remedial work on the frame in her father's memory. Messrs. Taylor & Co., bell founders of Loughborough, were asked to complete a survey when it was found that the joints of the bell frame were loose and some of the timbers were beyond repair. After dismantling the frame they discovered three sets of beams beneath. The top ones of 1775 were fairly sound and repairable, the middle set were much older and badly rotted. The bottom set was in reasonable condition. A new steel and iron girder frame was planned to hold the bells and distribute the weight more evenly within the tower.

On 12th March the bells were winched through the floor of the ringing chamber, laid in a row under the tower and then removed to Loughborough. The bells were away for more than a year. They were quarter turned and given new clappers which would consequently strike on a different part of the bells. The canons, by which the bells had been attached to their headstocks, were removed. The tenor was retuned, losing over 3cwt in the process. George Burton was subsequently presented with a pair of electric reading lamp standards made from a portion of the 1775 oak under the pit of the 6th bell for his approaching marriage to Miss Elizabeth S Bird.

The weights of the bells after their return from Taylors:

Treble	6-2-7	7	11-0-11
2	6-1-14	8	13-1-26
3	6-2-21	9	18-2-25
4	7-2-1	10	20-3-13
5	8-2-23	11	27-0-23
6	9-2-7	Tenor	37-3-15

Removing the bells, March 1924
Left to Right: D O Holme, Helen Bill, Charles Borrett, Douro T Potter and son,
Canon F Meyrick, George Burton, James Truman,?

The bells returned in May 1925. There is a story that as the tenor bell was being lowered into the new frame, a boy, Douro Potter's young son, Peter Mancroft Potter, enquired of his father 'Who do you think the bell will toll for first?' 'That, Peter', replied his father, 'we must leave. Who knows?' A couple of days passed and the boy asked 'Father, can you guess who you will toll the bell for?' 'No, Peter, no one can tell.' Within days, the bell tolled for the first time after its rehanging. It was tolled not by, but for, the beloved verger and steeplekeeper, Duoro Thomas Potter. Feeling unwell while ringing for Sunday service, he set his bell, sat down saying 'I shall have to stop!' His wife, in church, was summoned to the ringing chamber, but he was then unconscious and died in her arms of a heart attack. The vicar, ditching his prepared sermon, spoke affectionately of the verger, of his never-failing sense of humour and his vast knowledge of Mancroft's famed parishioner Sir Thomas Browne. An impressive crowd attended the funeral. It was the end of an era as the Potters had been sextons or vergers at Mancroft for generations - his great-grandfather Jonathan 1821 to 1841, his grandfather George, 1841 to 1868 and his father Douro Thomas Potter 1868 to 1893. By special request of

Potter's children, words of Sir Thomas Browne, excerpts of which their father would recite and read with the family every night, were incorporated in the funeral service. A brass plaque in the ringing chamber commemorates him, as does another fixed to the steps of the font which, together with its lofty cover, he and the vicar had recovered and returned to the original position.

Douro Potter under the tower with the bells

15

Ringing Revival

In 1927 the ringers revived the annual outing, hiring a 28 seater char-a-banc, to ring at Halesworth and Southwold, concluding the day with tea at Chapman's restaurant. They invited members of the congregation, hoping for new recruits since several capable ringers had left the city during the 1920s. One of these was J Armiger Trollope, ringer at Mancroft and other Norwich towers and later to move to London where he established himself as a notable historian of ringing. Once described as 'without doubt, the most gifted ringer of his age.'

The thirties saw the beginning of a ringing revival.

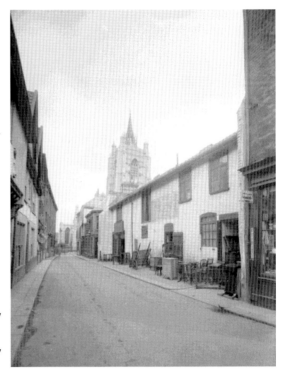

A view towards Mancroft in 1925 (before Bethel Street widened and City Hall was built)
(Image courtesy of Norfolk County Council Library and Information Service)

New Year's Eve was once more celebrated in style. In 1931 the vicar, the Revd H McMullen, treated the ringers and wardens to tea at the Café Royal near the church. Fred Knights, ringing master of the old company, was invited to rejoin the Mancroft ringers.

Ben Thompson, ringing master 1935-36, suffering from the effect of gas poisoning, was forced to give up. His loss was compensated by the arrival of Nolan Golden, one of the most competent ringers of his era. Mancroft bells were rung for coronation of King George VI in May 1937 and for the opening of the new City Hall in February 1939.

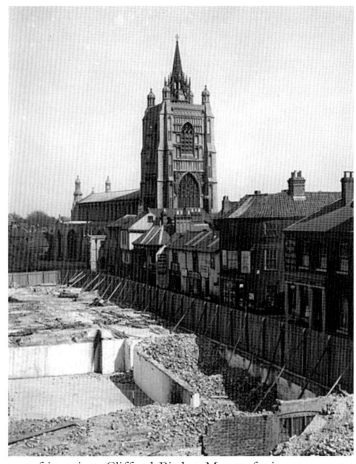

Demolition in progress, prior to the construction of the City Hall in 1935.
(Image courtesy of Norfolk County Council Library and Information Service)

The outbreak of war in September 1939 resulted in an almost complete cessation of ringing. By 1940 Mancroft members were down to eleven as some had joined the forces. In June that year ringing was banned completely, since the Ministry of Home Security decided bells should only be used as a warning in case of invasion. Clifford Bird, a Mancroft ringer, was a wartime police constable and one of his first jobs was to ascertain the state of the bells to make sure they could be rung or chimed in the event of invasion. However, bells were rung at occasional meetings with clappers tied.

Gilbert Thurlow, an enthusiastic, skilled ringer, was curate at Mancroft from 1939-1941 and found it a great disappointment that he never had the opportunity of ministering at Mancroft under normal conditions. He did not see the east window of mostly medieval glass, (removed during the war) never took a service after dark and never heard the Angelus or Sanctus bell. He wrote later 'I who take such an interest in England's ancient churches, their fittings and furniture should have nothing to add to Mancroft's furnishings but buckets, stirrup pumps and a fireman's ladder.' He and the Revd Mr Bridge, kept fire watch at night, sleeping in the tower. One night they were greatly disturbed when the inner part of the font cover collapsed. During heavy raids in April 1942 several windows were badly damaged; the west window on the south side almost completely demolished and a good deal of surface damage was done to the tower.

On 18th March 1943 during an air raid, firebombs landed on the nave roof, but were quickly extinguished. Daytime alerts interrupted some Sunday services and apparently the Revd Hugh McMullan's last sermon was preached in air raid warning conditions.

Ringing in the early 1950s, including visiting ringers:
Left to right: Arthur Bason, Cedric Curson, George Sayer, Stanley Coping, Gilbert Thurlow,
Bill Barrett, Edwin Goate, Noman Harding, Harry Tooke, Nolan Golden
(Image courtesy of the Eastern Daily Press)

Sadly, Ernest Palmer, one of the ringers, was killed by enemy action in April 1942. A brass plaque to his memory is fixed to the bookcase in the ringing chamber. The ban on ringing was lifted temporarily to celebrate victory at El Alamein in November 1942 and for Christmas that year and removed completely in June 1943. This led to considerable local publicity and attracted a number of learners, very necessary since Mancroft gradually lost many of the older members, in particular, John Burton, his brother George and Charles Borrett. On 19th February 1944, the BBC recorded a 'Home Flash' from Mancroft tower to be broadcast to the Middle East for Norfolk and Norwich men overseas. At the end of the war in 1945, the bells celebrated the triumph and joy of victory.

Arthur Bason was Ringing Master from 1939-1962. He and Nolan Golden attracted a number of new recruits. A few of us can remember some of this enthusiastic band: Cedric Curson, Bill Love, Charlie Goodman, Billy Barrett, Bert Gogle, a heavy bell ringer and self-taught pianist, George Sayer and his wife Gwen, nee Tunnadine, who rang her first peal at the age of 14. Clifford Bird, who, unable to continue with the police after the war as he had lost part of his foot in a motor cycle accident, joined the ambulance service. After retirement, he became a relief driver for a local limousine hire fleet, driving hearses and once chauffeuring royalty.

These were a tremendous group of ringers very active immediately before the war and for many years afterwards. They attempted all sorts of interesting methods, mostly composed and conducted by Nolan Golden.

These ringers were still very much in control in the early 1960s. I remember my first ringers' dinner at the Bell Hotel when we were expected to join in games such as musical chairs and pass the parcel: having a drink at the bar was frowned upon. Outings in the 1960s were by coach, echoing the days of the char-a-banc.

F Nolan Golden

Bert Gogle, Nolan Golden and Arthur Bason

On Sunday 2nd May 1965 the Guild rang a peal of 5040 Plain Bob Triples in 2 hours 55 minutes, to commemorate the 250th anniversary of the first peal in the tower in 1715 and in memory of those who took part in it:

Martin Cubitt	Treble	F Nolan Golden	5th
George Sayer	2nd	Clifford Bird	6th
David Cubitt	3rd	H William Barrett	7th
David R M Heighton	4th	F Charles Goodman	Tenor

Composed by Benjamin Annable
Conducted by F Nolan Golden

16
Learning the Ropes

Up until 1967, the ringers' annual dinners were maintained in the traditional format of the early twentieth century. Entertainment consisted of musical games with prizes, good food, crackers and little non-alcoholic drink. In 1968 the ringers' jug, at that time permanently on the table in the ringing chamber, was carefully conveyed to the Flixton Rooms and filled with beer - which immediately went flat! That year there were prolonged periods when no ringing was possible whilst the tower was strengthened and the new west window was installed in memory of the former incumbent, the Revd Frank Jarvis. The design of the tracery and glass, incorporated upturned mouths of bells and words from the advent hymn 'Wachet auf' (Wake O Wake).

Part of the tracery of the west window: note the figure in the top centre light is upside down.

By the 1970s the louvres were in need of repair. Wind was blowing in the rain and snow and pigeons fouled the belfry. On one occasion driving snow filled the bells which were in the 'up' position. It melted and the following Sunday the ringers were given a drenching! The church agreed to some weather proofing and the ringers volunteered to scrape and paint the bell frame. Between April and July 1975 on four nights of most weeks, work parties tackled the seemingly endless job. That year, in celebration of the bicentenary of the ring of 12 bells, the Family Service on St Peter's Day was conducted by Guild members. The following year, some pewter tokens belonging to the Ringers' Benefit Society turned up and their banner was found in the boiler room.

Mancroft bells have traditionally sounded over the city on national and civic occasions. A peal was rung for the royal wedding of Prince Charles and Lady Diana Spencer in June 1981. When the first royal baby was due, several ringers waited in the Bell Hotel for news brought by special messenger - no mobile phones in those days! By 10.30 that night they were ringing the back six bells for the birth of a son to Princess of Wales and thus were amongst the first in the country to welcome Prince William.

In 1985 Mancroft entered the National Twelve Bell Striking Contest for the first time. The eliminating round took place at St Peter's Nottingham. Mancroft ringers came last but felt they had done their best. However, they did win the Norwich Diocesan Association six bell competition and the Nolan Golden rose bowl graced the table in the ringing chamber (as it has done frequently over the years). That year the Steeple Keeper, somewhat remarkably, reported that there had been no new ropes fitted for ten years. Until new bell ropes were pre-stretched they were, by arrangement with the fire station, hung with weights in its practice tower for a time; but could, nonetheless, remain markedly elastic, as were the twelve which were fitted at the same time in 1986.

Richard Carter, affectionately known as 'Pike', owning to a certain resemblance to a television character in Dad's Army, was the ringing master in 1986, but resigned just after Christmas. A man of vision and high standards, frustrated that the bells were being rung without precision, that members were not taking the trouble to learn new methods and the 'same old people had yet again failed to look up a method relying on scrappy pieces of paper as an aid to memory'. However, Mancroft bells were too big a draw and he soon returned.

The clapper of the 11th bell broke the Sunday after Christmas in 1987, making an almighty thud as it hit the floor. Hurried repairs by a local blacksmith enabled the bell to sound again for New Year's Eve. Further inspection revealed that the 3rd, 4th and 5th required work.

Weather and pigeons were once again a problem. During March 1988 the bell chamber was completely cleaned out and eight sacks of bird droppings removed. Suddenly the bells were much more audible. Mancroft entered the National 12 Bell Striking Contest eliminator at Ipswich and were placed a creditable 4th.

Ringing for the birth of Prince Harry in 1984
Left to right: Paul Cubitt, George Sayer, Richard Carter, Martin Cubitt, Andrew Salisbury,
Cedric Curson, Clifford Bird
(Reproduced courtesy of the Eastern Daily Press)

17
The First Lady Ringing Master

Women had been ringing at Mancroft for about half a century, but it was not until March 1997 that the first lady Ringing Master was elected. Gill Knox ushered in a new era. Her aims were simple but positive: 'The maintenance of Sunday service ringing, a wider repertoire, a more unified, good-humoured atmosphere and improved striking.' These objectives proved very necessary when Neil Thomas, a former Ringing Master and Steeple Keeper at the time, suggested that the Guild should offer to host the National 12 Bell Contest in 1998, a first for Norwich. With her talent for organization, Gill set about the mammoth task of preparing for the competition day when ringers from all over the country would need to be catered for and entertained. A special brew of beer was to be had at St Andrew's Tavern and Mancroft ringers provided food. Practices were arranged and the best band selected from amongst the Mancroft ringers. The day was very successful and enjoyable, with the band coming 7th out of 8.

Peals to celebrate the 250th anniversary of the ringers' jug and the 400th anniversary of Kett's Rebellion kept the ringers on their toes. In addition, the clapper of the 11th broke and a new one was made, while fraying ropes need replacing and splicing.

That year David Brown was elected a member, one of the most talented ringers of our time, he was soon to play an important part in the life of both Gill and the Guild.

With a tenor bell weighing around two tons, ringing the back bells is a problem if sufficient muscle power is not available. To alleviate this situation, Clifford Bird, knowing the need for another bell, donated a light treble enabling a lighter ring of 10 to be rung, in memory of his parents in 1997. The first peal was rung on the new front ten, on 7th September 1997, to celebrate his 90th birthday.

Clifford died in May 2000. He had been Steeple Keeper at Mancroft for many years.

Clifford Bird with the new bell, 12 May 1997

In September 1998 a quarter peal was rung, half muffled, on the day of Princess Diana's funeral and in November a peal of Plain Bob Royal was rung in celebration of the Golden Wedding of HM Queen Elizabeth and HRH Prince Philip.

Gill was still Ringing Master at the Millennium. On New Year's Eve, after a party at her house, we made our way to the city centre. The festivities focused on the area by the City Hall and market. Crowds had already gathered as we made our way to the ringing chamber. As midnight approached, we stood in the circle, waiting for last few minutes. Keeping up an old tradition at Mancroft of ringing 'diminishing rounds', we started ringing as usual from the lightest to the heaviest then, beginning with the treble, each bell stopped in order until just the tenor was left to toll until the stroke of midnight. Then we rang the twelve. Even from high up in the tower, we could hear the cheers from the crowd below as the bells ceased. Later, from our vantage point, we watched the light and laser show as images were projected on the castle walls and lasers danced across the night sky. The following day we rang at noon along with many ringers throughout the country. We were filmed by the BBC, some of us appearing on national television. It is thought that nearly 5300 rings of bells were rung for the occasion and many new recruits were ready to help initiate the next thousand years of ringing.

An avid supporter of Norwich City Football Club, Gill arranged for us to ring as the team passed by the city hall celebrating becoming champions of Division One and promotion to the Premiership in 2004.

At the end of her three years in office, her deputy, Mike Roberts thanked her for her patience and good humour 'one of the few Masters to leave the Guild in a healthier state than when she started'.

David Heighton followed Gill as Ringing Master. He died suddenly just before the AGM at the end of his three year term of office; he had already written his report in which he had noted that we had rung for HM the Queen when she opened the Forum building, facing the west end of Mancroft across the Millennium Plain. Wonderful for the city, but the consequent loss of the car park made life difficult for ringers and congregation.

In 2006, Mancroft hosted an eliminator for the National 12 Bell Contest again organized by Gill Knox with the help of Trish Hitchins. This time Mancroft qualified for the final. Many Guild members supported them at the final at Worcester Cathedral, but unfortunately they were placed last. This event led to more commitment to improve the standard of striking and complexity of the methods rung. We were lucky that some experienced ringers had moved to Norfolk. David Brown undertook the selection of Mancroft's band for the National 12 Bell Contest and proposed to Gill.

Gill and David were married on 21st June 2008 at St Peter Mancroft, the reception being held at their beloved Norwich City Football Club. Just as Gill was speaking, the fire alarm went off and the building was evacuated. Gill played up to the situation by climbing into a fireman's cab and donning a helmet!

Gill and David's wedding at St Peter Mancroft

18

History Repeats

On 24th April 1925 the editor of *The Ringing World*, a national journal, wrote: 'A history of the bells of St. Peter Mancroft is almost a history of ringing in miniature'. How True! The challenges of method ringing, all the problems related to broken bells, clappers, ropes and stays, accidents in belfries and ringing chambers, disagreements and comradeship are there in every tower.

St Peter Mancroft claims many firsts in the world: the first peal, the first peal of Grandsire Triples and the first of Stedman. Its tower has played a major part in England's unique heritage, a heritage that is preserved in ringing today. Those who rang in the 1960s will remember Nolan Golden, who knew Ben Thompson who would have remembered J Armiger Trollope, who once wrote: 'I know Ben Smith, who knew John Trowse, who knew Chamberlin, who knew John Webster, one of Garthon's pupils.' Maybe 1715 was not all that long ago!

If John Garthon, the composer of that very first peal, could somehow be transported to the present, we could all ring together. Peal boards exist from his day, some sadly faded and dirty, including one of the long-length peal in 1737 that took more than eight hours to ring. Known as the 'Bloody Peal', it was a major achievement containing 12600 changes. In 1844 a long length of 7128 Stedman Cinques at Mancroft was reported in newspapers, nationally as well as locally. Garthon would probably be astounded to learn that four of our members today have rung some very long length peals: Mike Clements - one of 10080, taking over 5 hours, Simon Smith - three, the longest 18432, taking over ten hours. Simon Rudd - five, the longest 14688, more than 9 hours and David Brown - forty-two, the longest being 25560 changes taking over fourteen and a half hours!

Supposing we could turn back the clock and visit the tower in the time of John Chamberlin in 1772 after his band had just returned from York: we would ascend the same stone, spiral stairs. Our ringing chamber was just a storage room in his time. After several turns of rising steps, a narrow door opens on to the south aisle roof, the area covered in scratched signatures. It would have been a good place to wait a turn to ring and catch up with the gossip. The next narrow door, now blocked, was the entrance to their ringing chamber, half way up the west window. There was no view into the church in his day. During the 'ringing season' in the late afternoon from November to Christmas, the chandelier filled with candles was probably their only light. In 1889, a peal was finished in near darkness. Our nearest experience of this level of lighting occurred when we started to ring a peal on a winter's evening and forgot to put on the lights! As the dark descended we had to make do with the yellow floodlighting that produced long shadows, the ropes as silhouettes. (Six of us rang a peal by candlelight at St George Colegate fifty years ago, when the electricity failed.) I am sure Chamberlin would be delighted to know that four of us pensioners used our bus passes to go to York to commemorate his achievements in 1772.

Samuel Thurston, one of the most eminent ringers of his time, would have rung on the 1775 bells, as we do today. The sound he heard, we hear. He set the standard for the generations to follow. Nevertheless, in terms of peals, his opportunities were limited. He rang 36 peals, conducting all but seven and only two were rung at Mancroft. David Brown a member of the Guild, had already rung 4622 peals by June 2014. Also a member of Westminster Abbey Company, he has rung peals there for many Royal occasions including the Queen's Golden Jubilee and the wedding of Prince William to Katherine Middleton.

Douro Potter died in the ringing chamber in 1925, a man with an immense love for the church and its bells and a never-failing sense of humour. In 2007, Martin Cubitt, former Ringing Master, collapsed after calling some Stedman before a Sunday service. Paramedics arrived, but there was nothing that could be done. Like Douro, he had suffered a heart attack. Martin too had a wonderful sense of humour and gave so much of his time to music and bells. In his memory two 'spiders', to hook the ropes away when not in use, and wall boxes to hold the cleats, were fitted with suitably inscribed brass plaques.

New Year's Eve, was and is, an important occasion for Mancroft. Many visitors to the tower in the past have recorded their experiences in words and in art. About 1920, a visitor wrote 'It was on New Year's Eve that I climbed up the stairway into this famous ringing chamber. The stone polished by the hands of ringers ascending and descending during 500 years, is like burnished brass... The twelve ringers are again at the ropes; four of them women, one of them has come straight from a fancy dress dance in the brilliant colours of a Spanish peasant.' Fancy dress parties were regular for us during the 70s. Now it is generally a cosy gathering at the home of Sheila and Alan Spreadbury before ringing and we have given up 'firing' the bells.

Visitors have always been welcome, especially members of the congregation. In 2011 we opened the ringing chamber for the Norwich Heritage Open days and have done since then. We give demonstrations, explain the history and let one or two bells 'down' so they are safe for visitors to chime. 'Inspiring, fascinating, brilliant, awesome, can't believe this treasure is on our doorstep, so interesting, a real treat', are just a few of the comments made. In 2014, visitors numbered 335.

Visitors watching a demonstrations on a Heritage Open Day in 2013

The old ringers enjoyed their feasts and so do we. For many years now we have celebrated with a dinner in January. The church kindly subsidizes members and the vicar and churchwardens generally attend. The Ringing Master wears his badge of office and a speaker is invited. Usually previous members join us to share memories and catch up on activities.

Ringing outings have always been part of socializing. However, walking to York in the eighteenth century, pawning clothes and watches in order to get back to Norwich from Lavenham in about 1827, were rather more daring than today. In 1894 ringers took the train to London for an outing and we have done much the same since 2008, usually finishing the day with a curry in Brick Lane.

The 'Mancroft Project' to return the ringing chamber floor to its original eighteenth century position and create a heritage and teaching Centre beneath, has brought us together as a team. Many events are planned and some have happened, including a concert arranged by Anita Piper and Nikki Thomas.

The open-mouthed audience at the concert by musical Guild members which raised £750 for the Mancroft Project

Ringing is a fascinating, challenging hobby, with many traditions dating back to the seventeenth century. We ring some of the same methods in the same way, yet progress is a key to its survival. Those eighteenth century ringers rang very few peals, today Guild members, collectively, have rung many thousands.

The brazen lips of the bells have tolled for the dead, warned of invasions and proclaimed events. They have flung out laughter and joy for a new monarch, for feasts, for victories and happy occasions. They have shouted in triumph when wars have ended. They are part of our heritage to be preserved for future generations to enjoy.

Ringing Jargon Explained

Treble: The lightest bell, with the highest note, in any ring of bells.

Tenor: The heaviest bell, with the lowest note, in any ring of bells.

Rounds: Bells rung in a sequence of descending notes from Treble to Tenor, e.g. 123456 on six. Ringing normally starts and ends with Rounds.

Row: A sequence in which every bell strikes once.

Changes: The transitions between succeeding rows. Changes determine the structure of what is being rung.

Method: A specific sequence of changes. Methods all have unique names, e.g. Plain Bob, Grandsire, Stedman, Cambridge, and a suffix which indicates how many bells are involved:

5 Bells – Doubles	8 Bells – Major	11 Bells – Cinques
6 Bells – Minor	9 Bells – Caters	12 Bells – Maximus
7 Bells – Triples	10 Bells – Royal	

Peal: A set of at least 5000 changes, rung without repetition. A peal at St Peter Mancroft usually takes about 3½ hours of continuous ringing by one set of ringers.

Conductor: Person who takes responsibility for a piece of ringing, calling the necessary calls, checking and, if necessary, correcting the ringing.

Sources and Bibliography
Manuscript Sources

Norfolk Record Office (NRO)
Churchwardens' Accounts PD26/71-80
Ringers' Purse SO78/1-20
Notebooks by Philip Sadler SO 78/35, 733x2
Notebook and cuttings by Charles Borrett SO78/36, 733x2, SO78/39, SO78/48 733x2
Ringing at St Peter Mancroft 1785-1800 COL3/9
St. Peter Mancroft Guild of Ringers SO78
Samuel Thurston's notebook SO78/32 733x1
Charles Middleton's notebook SO205/1/4, 441x4

Newspapers and Journals
Norwich Gazette
Norwich Mercury
Norfolk Chronicle
Eastern Daily Press
York Courant
Ipswich Journal
Leicester and Nottingham Journal
Bell News
The Ringing World
Annual Reports of the Norwich Diocesan Association of Ringers

Books
Cattermole, Paul - *The Church Bells of Norfolk Part 6 Church and Other bells of Norwich* (The Golden Bell Press 2005)
Wratten, Cyril, compiler, Eisel John editor - *Order and Disorder in the Eighteenth Century. Newspaper Extracts about Church Bells and Bellringing* (Central Council of Church Bell Ringers 2010)
Eisel, John and Wratten, Cyril, compilers - *Order and Disorder in the Early Nineteenth Century. 1800-1829 Newspaper Extracts about Church Bells and Bellringing* (Central Council of Church Bell Ringers 2013)
Morris, Ernest - *The History and Art of Change Ringing* (Chapman and Hall Ltd. 1931)
Trollope, J Armiger - *The College Youths* (Woodbridge Press Ltd. Guilford 1937)
Meyrick, F J - *Round about Norfolk and Suffolk* (Jarrod & Sons Ltd. c.1925)
Eisel, John - *Giants Of The Exercise* (Central Council of Church Bell Ringers 1999)
Sanderson, Jean – *Change Ringing: The History of an English Art Volume 3* (Central Council of Church Bell Ringers 1994)

Part 2
GUILD CONTRIBUTIONS

The Purse
David Cubitt

LOVE AS BRETHREN is the motto distinguishable faintly atop the 'Articles Made & Agreed Unto December 22nd 1716 by the Society of Ringers in the City of Norwich for the ordering a Stock or Purse for the relief of such Persons as shall be therein concerned and shall stand-in need of the same…'. The Society of Ringers, the Norwich Scholars (scholars in the sense of students of the art and science of change-ringing), shared the motto, to be seen clearly on eighteenth century peal boards in the ringing chamber of St Peter Mancroft. The Articles numbered twenty-six. Article 1 dealt with the officers - a Headman, a Purser (treasurer), two Supervisors and two Feast Makers - and meetings, quarterly. Article 2 covered subscriptions - two shillings on election and two shillings quarterly until ten shillings paid and thereafter one shilling a quarter. Article 3 required candidates to have reached a defined standard in change-ringing. The Articles

continue with, for example, fines for absences; dismissal for certain offences; a requirement the supervisors hold no more than 20 shillings in hand; accounts to be made up and rendered every Whit Monday; an annual feast, also on Whit Monday; sickness benefit at 9 shillings six days after notice to the officers, thereafter 7 shillings a week for two months, after which 4 shillings a week; burial grant of 40 shillings; attendance at the funeral of a member. The extant Purse Book starts, by deduction, in 1739, the first three pages having been torn off. Names of the forty five members are stated, together with their payments. In 1740 treasurer held £110 0s 0d. The Purse also received donations from time to time from the Ringing Society, as £2 17s 9d in 1740 and £3 12s 6d in 1741. The feast in 1740, cost £1 19s 0d, included 46lbs of beef, 15lbs of mutton, 5lbs of veal, bacon, suet, 1 quart of butter, bread, pickle and pepper, plus tobacco, pipes, porterage and the assistance of a servant. The 1742 feast was held appropriately at Mr Ringer's in St Gregory's Parish, possibly the Blue Bell at the corner of Pottergate Street and Lower Goat Lane, which still stands, but as shop premises.

The Purse did not have a continuous existence, but was occasionally dissolved and restarted. In 1830 a successor 'Society or Club for the purpose of Practice and Improvement in the Science of Campanology as for raising and establishing a Fund for the Mutual Relief and Assistance' with its own rules was instituted. It met at the White Horse Inn, since demolished, on Hay Hill and was followed in 1865 by the 'St Peter Mancroft Ringers Benefit Society' which continued at the White Horse, where William Calcraft (1800 -1879), the chief hangman, regaled those other handlers of rope with tales of his experiences. Later the 'Society of Ringers (Norwich Scholars) Benefit Society' conducted its business at the Walnut Tree Shades, in Old Post Office Alley. The vicar of Mancroft, the Revd Frederick J Meyrick, barred the ringers from the tower in 1906 - he was also to cause the forced resignation of the organist two years later. The Norwich Scholars/Benefit Society members took themselves off to other towers and meeting places in the city. In 1923 the Benefit Society was finally dissolved, its assets divided among members. Some pieces of pewter originally owned by the Purse - a flagon, mugs and tokens have subsequently found their way to Mancroft. With its demise the Norwich Scholars passed into history.

The top of the parchment containing the articles of the Norwich Scholars

We should applaud the foresight of those ringers who, three centuries ago, appreciated that by unity and co-operation they could help one another in times of necessity.

Mancroft Music - 1775 and 1975
Tom Roast

The following notice appeared in the *Norwich Mercury* of 10th June 1775:

ST PETER'S BELLS
The peal of twelve will be first opened on Wednesday the 21st
of this instant, preceding which will be performed a grand
TE DEUM and JUBILATE, a Chorus from the Messiah,
and to conclude with the CORONATION ANTHEM.
The whole to be accompanied with a BAND of MUSIC.
The performance to begin at Eleven o'clock.
Admittance Three Shillings.

NB There will be a private REHEARSAL on Monday the 19th at Twelve o'clock precisely. Such Gentleman as will oblige the parish with their attendance are requested to attend at that time.

The band consisted of about thirty instrumentalists, together with the choir of Norwich Cathedral, and the music was performed to a 'genteel and numerous audience'.

MAY, 1869.

The works were probably all by Handel who was by far the most popular composer in England in the second half of the eighteenth century. It is likely that the first item was the *Dettingen Te Deum*, composed by Handel to mark a victory by British troops in 1743: it was performed two months later at a charity service in the Cathedral for the benefit of the Norfolk and Norwich hospital. The anthem was almost certainly *Zadok the Priest*.

The 1707 organ before it was moved from the west end.

The organist at Mancroft in 1775 was Edward Beckwith, a member of the influential family of Norwich musicians. Beckwith had been appointed to the post in 1769, replacing the blind organist, Samuel Cooke, who was considered to be unequal to his duties. But Beckwith, who was a lay clerk and master of the choristers at the cathedral, allowed Cooke to retain his position and salary, and acted as his deputy until Cooke's death in 1780. Edward Beckwith died in 1793 and was replaced as Mancroft organist first by his son John Christmas Beckwith, and then by his grandson, John Charles Beckwith.

Two hundred years later:

St Peter's Day, Sunday 29th June 1975, was earmarked for celebrating the bicentenary of the ring of twelve. At the time Mancroft was experiencing an interregnum, the Reverend Bill Westwood having just left to take up the position of Bishop of Edmonton. The Family Service at ten o'clock was entirely taken by ringers. The responses were led by Barbara Payne, the lessons read by Clifford Bird and Nolan Golden, separated by a touch on handbells, and David Heighton led the prayers. There were two addresses: David Cubitt spoke on 'Mancroft bells' and Andrew Salisbury on the 'Spiritual Implications of Bell Ringing'. The duties of organist were shared by Tom Roast, who played Mendelssohn's *Prelude in C minor* before the service, and Martin Cubitt, the Ringing Master, whose final voluntary was J S Bach's *Prelude and Fugue in B minor* BWV544.

At Evensong the preacher was the Very Reverend Gilbert Thurlow, Dean of Gloucester, past president of the Central Council of Church Bell Ringers, and author of *Church Bells and Ringers of Norwich*. The choir sang Purcell's anthem *Rejoice in the Lord, Alway*, generally known as the 'Bell' anthem for its opening bars of descending scales. Following the service there was a concert of music typical of two hundred years earlier. It was performed by the Academy of St Thomas, conducted by Ivan Cane, and the Mancroft choir, directed by the organist and choirmaster, Kenneth Ryder. All of the music was by Handel: the piece known as 'The Arrival of the Queen of Sheba' from *Solomon*; his coronation anthem *My heart is inditing*, the organ concerto in D minor, and the last of the Opus 6 grand concertos.

A Limited Number of Ladies
Janet House

When the St Peter Mancroft Guild of Ringers decided to recruit ladies to the band in 1916 they were behind the times. Women were ringing regularly in many parts of the country in the later years of the 19th Century and in 1896 Miss Alice White of Basingstoke rang the first tower bell peal by a lady, only days after having been tossed by a bull! (In those long ago days, women, like the clergy and the military, were given the courtesy of a title in ringing reports, a practice which died out after 1945.)

The new recruits at Mancroft made great strides and by May 1919 the *Eastern Daily Press* was reporting that the Misses Helen and Frances Bill had rung plain courses of Grandsire Cinques, adding, 'few ladies in England can ring a touch on twelve bells'.

That year church bells rang out across the country to celebrate the peace. Slipped in amongst the peals was one of Grandsire Triples at Knebworth in Hertfordshire. It was the first for the ringer of the second bell, a Miss May Durrant, who 'hails from Norwich'. Twelve days later the St Peter Mancroft Guild rang a peal of Plain Bob Major at St John de Sepulchre. May Durrant rang the third, her older sister Hilda rang the second and Frances and Helen Bill rang the fourth and fifth bells, the first peal at the first attempt for these three. Women's peal ringing had come to Norwich.

Six months later, on 28th December 1920, May rang the first peal by a woman at St Peter Mancroft, a peal of Plain Bob Royal. She was 22 at the time and it took 3 hours and 38 minutes to ring. She rang another, the first peal of Stedman Caters by a local band, the following April, and then disappears from the peal lists at Mancroft for ever. This was not uncommon among early women ringers. May married in 1922 and it may be that, in those days, marriage and children limited some women's ringing careers. Not, however, that of Mrs George H Cross (maiden name unknown) who, with her husband, rang the first peal on the bells by a married couple in 1931.

In contrast Miss Helen Bill, also recruited during the War years, became a stalwart of the Mancroft Guild. She was ringing in quarter peals of Stedman Cinques in 1922 and went on to ring six peals at Mancroft, including one of Kent Treble Bob Maximus in 1926. This was the first time a woman had rung a peal here in which all twelve bells were ringing changes, and would probably have been rare anywhere in the country. Helen continued ringing until her death in 1946.

The years leading up to the Second World War saw women ringing regularly at Mancroft. Among the new ringers was Gwen Tunnedine who married another leading Mancroft ringer, George Sayer. In November 1944, Gwen took part in a half-muffled peal on the death of William Temple, the beloved Archbishop of Canterbury. As 'Mrs George Sayer', she was the first woman to appear on a peal board in the tower, and the only one to be given a title. Gwen is still remembered with affection.

The Second World War proved to be a watershed. Before 1945, 11 women had rung in 28 of the 150 peals rung at Mancroft, and they were predominantly members of the local band. Since 1945 the majority of women peal ringers have been visitors, including many well known in ringing circles. Among the early ones were Claudia Harding, later Critchley, from Kings Lynn, who rang here in the early 1950s, and Olive Rogers. Trish Hitchins, a member of the present band and Olive's daughter, remembers being looked after by her grandparents at their farm in Suffolk while her parents came to Norwich to ring. Doris Lidbetter, who, coincidentally, introduced Olive to ringing, moved to Acle and rang seven peals here in the late 1950s.

It's probably true to say that since the 1960s there have been few peals at Mancroft without at least one female member of the band. The majority have rung only one peal suggesting that, for many, the prospect of a second peal at Mancroft is like the prospect of a second marriage was to Samuel Johnson, 'the triumph of hope over experience'. Nevertheless there have been some remarkable ringing achievements. In 1986, a visiting band from the Society of Royal Cumberland Youths rang a peal of Bristol Maximus on the bells, with the front four bells rung by women. In 1993, another visiting ringer, Angela Beardow, rang in a peal of 15 Spliced Maximus. Bells are hung in such a way that ringers do not need to be hefty themselves to ring, but skill and stamina are essential, especially for women ringing heavy bells. The late Alison Regan, who can only be described as slight in build, rang the eleventh bell to two peals of Stedman Cinques.

The eleventh weighs 27cwt, the equivalent of 16 men. In 2008, Claire Roulstone rang the tenor to peal of Stedman Cinques. This bell weighs nearly 38cwt, the equivalent of 23 men or a Ford Transit van, and Claire rang it for 3 hours and 41 minutes without stopping. Both are remarkable ringers and Alison is greatly missed.

Women have played a full part in the development of local ringing at Mancroft in the past 20 years, and much of this is thanks to Gill Knox. Gill was Secretary to the Guild, and the first woman Master in 1997. She took part in the first, and as yet only, quarter peal, 'by an all ladies band on these bells' in March 1995; with Trish Hitchins and Faith Pearce, she rang in the first local peal of Bristol Maximus in 2012; and she is one of only three women to have rung more than 20 peals on the bells.

Of the present 29 Guild members, 10 are women, with differing ringing experiences and ages spanning five decades. Some of the younger ones are busy producing the next generation of Mancroft ringers! By making the bells easier to ring, raising the ringing room floor would certainly encourage an all ladies peal on the bells, and might also mean that the older members of the present band could look forward to ringing a peal in 2020 to celebrate the centenary of May Durrant's remarkable achievement.

Postscript:

In 1911 an over-enthusiastic curate in Dagenham banned women from the belfry because he thought it an unsuitable place for ladies. His actions produced a flurry of letters in *The Ringing World* most condemning his action, but one supporting the ban for three reasons:

'1. They (women ringers) will do men out of their hobby.

2. They will be given all the privileges, while the gentlemen ringers will have to "take a back seat" and look on.

3. They will do as the Vicar of Quorn (Leicestershire) once said: "Cause all the trouble."'

'A limited number of ladies' at Mancroft have proved him wrong!

Memories from the 1960s
Andrew Salisbury (Ringing Master 2005)

I first came to Mancroft on my birthday in 1967 (I won't say which birthday but I was younger then).   I particularly remember a big welcome from Martin Cubitt and Nolan Golden.

One of my first experiences was being taken by Nolan up to see the bells at night time. The lighting up there was hardly superb and the safety installations were rather primitive. Any way we saw and heard the bells ringing standing on the plank above the tenor! I must say that it left a lasting impression and it may not be a surprise that I now have two hearing aids.

I would like to mention three ringers, especially Bert Gogle who was a fascinating person to talk to, Billy Barrett who was a fine ringer and very helpful and Leslie Bailey was always ready to ring peals and I rang some very good ones with him.   I have avoided talking about present day ringers.

Nolan Golden will always be remembered for his beautiful handwriting and his peal compositions, however, he did have a maverick side to his nature on occasions.   I remember once when I was ringing the tenor to Yorkshire Maximus, he was conducting from the treble and I saw him jump [deliberately I think] from 9th place to 6th place and then try for several minutes to put the bells right again.   When I became Secretary of the Norwich Diocesan Association he gave me a lot of help and support.

There were times when some dissention was apparent in the ringing chamber and the vicar, Bill Westwood, always relished coming to the Guild's annual meeting. He said it was worse than the annual meeting of the flower arrangers at St Margaret's Lowestoft! I had to see him about ringing and he asked me what the most valuable thing in the church was. I suggested the bells or the east window and Bill modestly replied 'Me'.

I was Secretary of the Guild for two stints and these passed very smoothly I think. When I was Ringing Master, the National 12 Bell Striking Contest was being held at Mancroft and I decided to enter the Guild for the competition. There was quite a bit of organising required for the day and for the ringers who came to practise and the event tended to be a low key occasion. We did have two volunteers from the congregation who arranged refreshments in the Octagon. The organisation now is very different. Ever since then we have had Ringing Masters who have kept the ringing going - most impressive!

Memories of a Past Steeple Keeper from the 1970s
Steve Day

I have been steeple keeping for around forty five years, firstly in Essex, then in Norfolk and Suffolk. My trade is a diesel engineer which has been very useful in understanding the mechanics of bells. From 1977 I looked after the six bells of St George Colegate and the five bells of All Saints in Norwich. I assisted the then Mancroft Steeple Keeper, Malcolm Brown, and took over in 1985. In 1987 work took me to Suffolk where I looked after the bells at Beccles. Back in Norwich in 1994 I returned as Steeple Keeper in 2001. I stood down from Mancroft in 2010 but still look after St George Colegate and the redundant towers in the care of the Norwich Historic Churches Trust.

In 1924 the bell fittings were restored. Due to the size of the timbers required in the old eighteenth century wooden frame, several of the bells had been hung in the windows. This resulted in some of the bells shouting, in particularly the eleventh which was nick-named 'bully boy' by the market traders. Taylors of Loughborough designed a very clever frame constructed from iron 'H' frame sides and a rolled steel joist base. This bought all the bells within the tower and evened out the sound. They also fitted steel headstocks, hasting stays and ball-bearings to all the bells.

In 1965 the tenor clapper came out and damaged the 11th frame. Fortunately the frame is constructed like a massive meccano set so replacing the frame side was fairly simple.

The biggest problem at Mancroft is the stretch in the ropes. In the 1970s we pioneered the use of polyester rope instead of the traditional hemp. Initially there were problems with chaffing but after refacing and waxing the pulleys it proved very successful. In 1985 I noticed several of the bearings were showing wear. The original 1924 bearings were obsolete so Taylors were commissioned to replace the gudgeons with metric sizes allowing modern bearings to be fitted. They also replaced the metal clapper bearing bushes (that were impossible to grease) with maintenance free polyethylene. The pulleys were reconditioned and adjusters were added to the 9th to cure the odd-struckness (with rather limited success).

The drawback of polyester rope is its incredible strength. In 2003 a splice failed on the 8th bell. The loose end managed to tie itself in a perfect knot around the top guide 45 feet above, and damaged the wheel. The wheel was soon mended but despite all our efforts with poles and hooks we could not get the rope untied. I had to call in a favour from local builder and ringer, Gerry Kelly. We had to use a thatching ladder from the ground, through the ringing floor and on to the top guide approximately 70 feet and untie it. Following this I modified all the splices to prevent a reoccurrence. We were ringing on practice night in 2010 when the tenor clapper broke. The resulting boom as the lump of wrought iron hit the floor under the bells caused the tenor ringer to let go of his rope so we had a rope with 1½ tons behind it, thrashing around the tower. It looked like it was going to pick the table up or worse, rip the guide out of the wall so I told (shouted at!) everyone to evacuate the tower. As well as being concerned for their safety, I wanted somewhere to run to if required! I managed to get hold of the rope and bring the bell under control with no damage. The clapper was taken to the Whitechapel Bell Foundry who forged the two parts together again.

Bellringers and Beer
Martin Howe (Ringing Master 1976-1979)

There has always been an association between bellringers, pubs and beer. The Mancroft ringers, for example, have a ringers jug in the Treasury.

Many ringers up and down the country find an answer to their thirst with a visit to a nearby hostelry following a practice or at the conclusion of a long spell of ringing. These gatherings not only provide the chance to socialize, and discuss various matters, but also gives the opportunity to entertain and get to know visiting ringers.

Over recent years, after practice, St Peter Mancroft ringers have engaged in the habit of moving from one pub to another at fairly regular intervals. Most of these being within walking distance of the church and too many to name and describe.

Going back many decades, in the early-mid nineteenth century when ringing was physically much harder than it is today and a male dominated occupation, the quenching of thirst was a serious business. About this time, the Walnut Tree Shades was the provider of the welcome liquid. The pub, still operating in Old Post Office Court, was licensed in 1841. Cabinet makers also used the pub and it has been suggested that through this connection, the probability of the pub acquiring its name, although there is no hard and fast evidence to prove this.

We can briefly look at the history of the hostelry Mancroft ringers use today, The Coach and Horses. The pub in Bethel Street dates back to 1710 although parts of the building go back to 1200. On the wall outside there is a parish marker indicating the pub lies between the parishes of St Giles Church and that of St Peter Mancroft. An old ascension tide custom took place years ago of 'beating the bounds' whereby choir boys from both parishes were 'bumped and dusked' along the boundaries to ensure they would remember where their parish ended!

With the parish marker it is possible to enjoy a pint or two in both parishes and leave the custom of 'beating the bounds' to others.

The bells of St Peter Mancroft have no boundaries. Their glorious sound and message ring loud and clear across each adjoining parish and beyond.

Reflections of a Former Ringing Master
Gill Knox (1997-2000)

My first glimpse of ringing was aged 5 when I was carried up the tower stairs of Wymondham Abbey by the curate's wife. I was fascinated by the colourful ropes bobbing up and down in this hidden part of the church and was disappointed that I was too little to have a go.

I learnt to ring aged 11, taught by Tom Spight and Harry Tooke on the pretext of gaining my Girl Guide badge. Tom and Harry were two venerable retired gents who were Wymondham Abbey institutions but like chalk and cheese. Tom was a gentle and charming man, very kind with endless patience. Harry was an irascible Norfolk character who loved to regale people with gory WWI tales and regarded anyone from out of the County as a foreigner. He either liked you or he didn't but he was always very kind to me.

I rang my first peal in 1977 at Hethersett conducted by another famous ringing veteran, Billy Barrett. I didn't ring my second peal until 10 years later but have rung around 300 since. I did little ringing at University but when I moved back to Norwich in 1987, I started ringing at St Peter Mancroft.

Mancroft at that time was a rather daunting place at first visit and not overly welcoming. There was a culture of shouting during touches (often to make yourself heard) and the Guild was full of strong characters with strong opinions. That said, everyone was very kind to me and forbearing once they realised I was prepared to stick at it and ring twice on Sunday.

I served variously as Secretary and Deputy Ringing Master and still have the official Deputy Ringing Master's garter that Martin Cubitt made especially for me as a badge of office.

I was elected the first lady Ringing Master in 1997. I understand there was the odd abstention in the vote and afterwards one Guild member drew me aside to ask me what my plans were for the belfry. When I told him eagerly 'some new curtains and scatter cushions' he looked rather horrified! However the Guild are a very loyal bunch with many members who have already done a stint as a Guild officer so they understand the difficulties and I received a huge amount of support and co-operation.

The EDP got wind of my election so on a slow news day sent a reporter round to take a picture and interview me producing almost a full page article – the picture was OK but I lied about my age even though I was only 35!

My aim as Ringing Master was to maintain and improve striking, introduce new methods and above all improve the rather tense at times atmosphere, with less shouting, more tolerance and good humour. I tried to be as welcoming as possible to visitors but it's always a difficult balance between accommodating newcomers to 12 bell ringing and maintaining the quality of ringing. It's not an easy job being Ringing Master managing a group of volunteers of all ages and personalities and it's impossible to keep everyone happy.

During my tenure we had the usual dinners and outings etc. we entered the 12 Bell eliminator and also hosted one successfully at Mancroft – getting through to the final.

Clifford Bird donated the extra treble to make a light ten and we had a brass plaque engraved to commemorate it – unfortunately we got the spelling of the Latin inscription wrong so after the official unveiling we had to have it done again on the other side!

We rang a quarter peal on the morning of Princess Diana's funeral which rang out over what seemed like a ghost town and we rang a peal for the funeral of The Queen Mother.

We also rang in the new Millennium and went onto the church roof to watch the enormous crowds whose revelries completely drowned out the bells. We cracked opened bottles of champagne in the belfry sending corks flying into and lodging into the nave ceiling.

The absolute best thing that happened to me during my time as Ringing Master was meeting my husband David Brown. David is reputed to be the best living ringer in terms of his all round ringing abilities and achievements so it was quite a coup when he moved to Norfolk and started to visit Mancroft. I knew little about him when he first turned up and would give him a line of something relatively simple and ask him to learn it for next week. He is a very modest chap and assured me he had done his homework and probably didn't need anyone standing behind him.

Anyway to cut a long and romantic story short we finally got married at Mancroft in 2008 following a heavy hint I dropped in one of my annual dinner speeches. All the Guild members were invited to the wedding at St Peter Mancroft and we had a reception at Norwich City football ground which resembled the aftermath of a 12 bell striking competition. I believe we were only the second pair of Guild members to get married at Mancroft after David and Mo Cubitt in 1963. We are, along with the Guild, living happily ever after…..

The Clifford Bird Bell

First Impressions
James Hughes

I arrived at St Peter Mancroft for the first time, with the image in my head of a painting I have in a book, of the ringing room in the eighteenth century, showing a quite barren room situated near the top of the west window with one or two peal boards on the wall. I didn't really know what to expect when I arrived. Not having done any 12 bell ringing for about twenty years, and then only fitfully, I suppose what I really wanted was to find a struggling band who would be so glad of an extra pair of hands that they would not notice my shortcomings. No such luck! What I found, on entering what must be the warmest ringing gallery north of the Alps, was an equally warm welcome from a far from struggling band. I counted 26 ringers on my first visit. They rang, amongst other things, Cambridge and Bristol Maximus. I started attending regularly in October 2013 after an initial visit in August before moving to the area, and I was impressed that even with so many ringers I was remembered from my previous visit. I have found a very well run set-up with not only a proficient band off ringers but also a well organised social calendar and a sense of community. I am honoured and excited to be a part of this illustrious and venerable society.

Being a Steeple Keeper
Ben Trent

I am joint Steeple Keeper, along with Pete Sawyer, at St Peter Mancroft. I have been helping to look after the bells for about 5 years. I do not come from an engineering background nor do I claim to know what I am doing all of the time! I help to look after the bells because of my willingness to learn and interest in how things work. Getting hands on experience with such a historical set of bells and knowing that I am partially responsible for keeping them ringing, fills me with a great sense of pride. I have helped with a number of tasks over the years, mostly ropes. The tail ends (where they wear out) are often re-spliced to help them last as long as possible, which depending on the quality of the rope can vary widely! I have helped with fitting new pulley boxes to the back bells, to help make them easier to handle. I have helped to change stays on some bells and have even helped to fit a clapper to the tenor, which took two of us to lift! Through all of this and other general maintenance, there is plenty to be kept busy with and plenty for me to take in.

The Lincolnshire Experiment 1995
Eric Hitchins

There are two major factors in achieving a high standard of bell ringing, the bells and the ringers.

For many years the 'Mancroft Band' had practised and achieved a good result in a limited number of methods with, generally, Cambridge being the most difficult, and in order to progress beyond that, it was considered, that of all of the other methods which could be 'tried' Lincolnshire would provide a new challenge.

The objectives were quite clear, to widen the repertoire of methods rung, to assist with learning the method, to establish a surer rhythm and a higher standard of ringing especially for Sunday Service Ringing.

It was Bill Jackson, a highly regarded and experienced member of the Band who proposed an alternative approach to learning using handbells. The ringers would meet in the tower and other venues when 12 members would team together, each using one handbell, and endeavour to simulate the experience of ringing the method as they would on tower bells in perhaps less demanding physical circumstances.

There were eight 'meetings' of the groups during which there were also quizzes on the method, assistance with learning techniques and other training aids and the opportunity to compare personal experiences with other group members

The outcome of all of this endeavour is reflected in the success of the four quarter peals which were rung, two at St Peter Mancroft and two at Great Yarmouth and on general ringing on other occasions

The other noticeable outcome - all of the participants were presented, by Bill, with a t-shirt with its own Lincolnshire logo!

The Bristol Project
Trish Hitchins

Aimed at advancing and widening our 12 bell ringing, the Bristol Project was led and motivated by Guild member Simon Rudd. We were already ringing the basic Surprise Maximus methods, Cambridge, Yorkshire and Lincolnshire, on a regular basis along with Grandsire and Stedman Cinques, but Bristol is more difficult and represented a big step up. It all started in 2007 when Simon arranged a number of Saturday evening 12 bell practices away from Mancroft, mainly on the easier twelve at Great Yarmouth, with the specific purpose of practising Bristol Maximus. Nearly all the Mancroft band took part and a large number learnt and practised Bristol Maximus for the first time. These evenings were all followed by enjoyable meals and socializing in the Gallon Pot. The practices continued into 2008 when a couple of quarter peals were rung and it culminated on July 22nd 2012 when eleven members of the local band, along with one friend, rang in a peal of Bristol Maximus at Mancroft. As a result of this project, Bristol Maximus has become part of our regular Sunday and practice night repertoire at Mancroft. Striving together towards this common goal, was both challenging and enjoyable and it helped us bond together as a stronger band. From a personal viewpoint, this was a massive personal achievement, giving me great motivation, enjoyment and a huge sense of satisfaction. I never, ever thought that this was something I would achieve, let alone after the big 60 and having been ringing for 50 years! So - it's never too late if you really want to achieve something!

Socializing at Yarmouth after a Bristol Practice

Some Ringing Recollections
David Brown

I've been a bellringer for some 50 years now. My 'home tower' is the magnificent church of St Peter Mancroft in Norwich and I am also a member of the band at Westminster Abbey in London. What initially brought me to ringing at the tender age of 10? I recall that the first time I ever set foot inside a tower was at Langley Marish in Berkshire, where my parents lived. One day my father and I were walking past the church and ran into an elderly man whom we recognised as a member of the congregation. He said that he was just going up the tower to wind the clock and did we want to come and have a look? From the moment I entered the ringing chamber and saw the brightly coloured sallies hanging down I was fascinated. We went through the mysterious intermediate chamber redolent with the smell of old timber with the huge clock gently ticking away and the ropes drawn in chutes hither and thither and on up to the bells themselves. To my young eyes they seemed huge and I marvelled at how it might be possible for the ringers so far below to control the bells. The clock winder said that if I was interested I should come along to watch on a practice night. So I did! The ringers were friendly and asked if I wanted to learn. I leaped at the chance and I have never regretted it. My perseverance in the early stages was I am sure unrelated to the fact that an extremely attractive girl of my age was also learning to ring. I was normally too tongue-tied and gauche to pluck up the courage to speak to her!

The ringers at Langley only rang fairly basic things and my introduction to change ringing occurred somewhat fortuitously. I had started at Slough Grammar School when I was aged 11 and noticed that there were two brothers – one in my year – who wore bell-shaped badges on their lapels. I asked the younger boy what they signified and he told me that it meant that they belonged to the Oxford Diocesan Guild of Church Bellringers. He said that they rang at Slough where they were learning to 'hunt'. I hadn't got a clue what he meant by this, thinking maybe there was some link between ringing and chasing small animals. A visit to Slough tower for a Friday practice soon enlightened me! The tower captain at the time was an absolute enthusiast for ringing called Bill Birmingham and he seemed to adopt me as a project. After he had got me out of some bad habits in terms of how I handled the rope and following some fairly disastrous early attempts at 'method ringing', I eventually got the hang of it. Bill was responsible for getting me into some of my early peals.

As some will know, a peal involves some three hours of continuous ringing and is quite a tiring and mind-sapping feat to accomplish. I have now rung over 4,600 of these, but I can remember how daunting those first ones were. There seemed to be an awful finality when all were assembled and the tower door was firmly shut and locked against any distracting intrusion. I recall a distinct sense of claustrophobia. However, that was soon banished when the ringing began and the need to concentrate overcame the fears. Some of my early peals were with a redoubtable character from Oxford called Alan Pink, who had an awe-inspiringly large physical presence and a short fuse when it came to people making mistakes in his peals. This was a powerful incentive to concentrate and not to be humiliated by being barked at! I recall that Bill used to drive me up to the Oxford area for those peals. Afterwards, the ringers would usually repair to a pub but at that time pubs were rarely keen to admit children and in case my parents were vehemently anti-alcohol. So I was usually relegated to waiting outside while one of the adults brought me out a glass of lemonade. Over time the lemonade was added to with a dash of beer and then half beer and half lemon to make shandy. Eventually around the age of 16 – and quite illegally – I graduated to beer and started entering pubs!

I was just 14 when I joined the well-known London based ringing organisation known as the Ancient Society of College Youths. Since I first started reading the ringers' newspaper 'The Ringing World' and learning more about the wider world of ringing, I had become fascinated by this ancient organisation, founded in 1637. I was aware that they rang at some venerable London towers such as St Paul's Cathedral, St Mary-le-Bow and Westminster Abbey and that some of the best ringers in the land belonged to the Society. It was a thrill to be elected and I started going to practices after school on a Tuesday night from the age of about 16. A year or so later I had the privilege of being asked to go and ring at St Paul's Cathedral on a Sunday, and for a couple of years until I went to university I spend every other Sunday in London ringing there morning and afternoon. I was in awe of some of the ringers I met in London at this time. One was a man called Jack Crampion, who was then in his 60s and who was old enough to have rung with one of the greatest ringers of all time, Bill Pye back in the 1920s. Then there was Philip Chalk, an imposing figure, who was a consultant surgeon and looked and dressed like a man from the Edwardian age. There can be few ringers today who ring heavy bells dressed in suit trousers, a waistcoat and tie.

When I went to university at Oxford in 1971, I started ringing peals in earnest, although I did find some time for university work. One year I recall that I was leading peal ringer with a then record number of 177 peals in the year. I sometimes ask myself why I have rung so many peals. I suppose it is for a mix of reasons, although the ones which are prominent have varied over the years. In the early years I think like a lot of prolific ringers I had a numbers obsession. The more peals I could ring the better! No doubt there is a competitive and collecting streak here! A very significant attraction is the mental challenge. One good thing about ringing is that there are always new things to tackle, however experienced you are, and some of the peals rung today are probably close to the limits of human competence. To take part in something which requires total mental concentration for three hours or more and achieve success is very rewarding. One of the additional challenges which I enjoy is conducting peals. All peals require a conductor in order to navigate to a successful conclusion and many of the compositions I have called have presented a significant mental challenge on top of actually taking part in the ringing itself.

Also very important of course is enjoyment of the noise that one is making! To have the privilege of ringing a peal on a fine set of bells costing a huge sum of money in the magnificent settings of a cathedral is something that is granted to few people and is such a rewarding experience. Lastly, but perhaps most important, is the social side of ringing. There's the sense of teamwork where a band of ringers is working well together to ring a good peal, as well as the enjoyable social session in the pub afterwards. Most of my best friends are, it goes without saying, bellringers. I met my lovely wife Gill through ringing when she was Ringing Master at St Peter Mancroft after I first moved to Norwich in the late 1990s.

It is difficult looking back on 50 years of ringing to single out particular highlights as there have been so many memorable occasions. Some of the achievements I most treasure have involved 'long lengths' taking much longer than three hours in order to set records in different methods. My longest was some 14 hours of continuous ringing at All Saints Worcester back in the 1980s when I was involved in a successful attempt for the longest peal of a method called Bristol Surprise Maximus. Also memorable, but for the wrong reasons, was an attempt for an even longer peal at Bradford Cathedral, also in the 1980s, which would have taken over 17 hours if successful. Sadly, we failed after over 14 hours of ringing when mental tiredness caused a fatal error! More happily, I recall peals at some of the country's great churches It was awe-inspiring to ring a peal at Liverpool Cathedral when I was still a teenager. As some will know, the cathedral is a huge structure and the bells – the heaviest ringing peal in the world – are on a scale to match. The peal took well over four hours and I was exhausted afterwards. Over the years I have also ring a number of peals on the superb bells at York Minster. Many would claim these as the best 12 and, indeed, the noise they make is as overwhelming and sumptuous as listening to a great organ.

Bellringing has for me been a great hobby, as well as a way of providing a service to the church. Even after all these years and all those peals, I still enjoy it hugely and am always finding new challenges to tackle. It saddens me that fewer young people are coming forward in the modern era to learn to ring. If only they knew what they could get out of it, there would be queues of people wanting to learn! I hope that the plans we have at Mancroft for a ringing teaching centre will play an important part in helping to reverse this trend.

Extracts from Ringing Master's Reports at the Guild AGM
Jon Spreadbury (Ringing Master 2009-2012)

2010

Ringing over the past year has been generally well attended and it does the Guild great credit that we are able to produce good ringing on 12 for both Sunday morning and evening services most weeks. For a city the size of ours, and with bells as challenging as ours, I feel this is a great achievement and I thank all members of the Guild for this. Monday practices seem to have verged from the sublime to the ridiculous! At one stage we were getting in excess of 30 people on a Monday, which meant that people were not getting as much of a ring as they would have liked. Numbers seem to have now dropped down to a more manageable level, and I think the level of ringing has improved as a result.

Having said this, part of the reason the numbers have been so high is that, as the only 12 bell band in the county, any ringers with aspirations of ringing on 12 need to come to Mancroft to learn how 12 bell ringing works. Sometimes we are very fortunate that Surprise Maximus ringers move to the area, but we also need to train the next generation. It should be noted, though, that the band does now include more young ringers, albeit 'young ringers' describes those under 40.

There have been five peals rung on the bells this year, Stedman by a visiting ASCY band in July, Bristol Major on the back 8 by a predominantly Guild band with Alan Regin on the tenor, Grandsire Cinques by a Guild band in memory of Caroline Harris in November, Cambridge Maximus by a 'Guild plus friends' band in January, and Grandsire Cinques by a Guild band for dinner day in memory of Stanley Gall. This shows that, with leadership and encouragement, this time primarily from Simon Rudd, and application and enthusiasm from the Guild members, we are capable of ringing, not just to a high standard, but to a very high level of skill too. Certainly friends outside the area have been very impressed with what has been achieved here over the last few years.

Jon as Santa's little elf

The Guild dinner was once again held at Park Farm in Hethersett. As usual the food was excellent and the service from the staff first class. Our guest speaker was Revd. Paul Cubitt, which on a personal level was lovely because, in a previous life when Paul was a Sales Rep and I had hair, Paul was a mainstay of the St Albans band I rang with, and he was a major part of my ringing development. Paul delivered a thought provoking and entertaining speech, which had the unexpected side effect of everyone counting the stairs on the way up to the ringing room the next morning. My thanks go to Eric and Richard for their organization of the meal, and to the church for their continued support of the event.

Mancroft Guild Dinner 2011
Left to Right: Simon Rudd, Neil Thomas, Tim Joiner, David Brown, Richard Turk,
Owen Winter, Jon Spreadbury and Faith Pearce

2011

One thing that really pleases me with the Guild is the attitude of the members. If someone has a good idea, they tend to now run with it and make it happen. We have seen it with the 2015 Project and last summer most of the Guild enjoyed a lovely summer's afternoon at Hethersett. The idea was an intra-society striking competition within the Guild, pitting members of the College Youths against the Cumberland Youths against those who were neither. The result was a fun afternoon of good ringing, the College Youths winning the Triples part of the competition but the Cumberlands triumphing overall. The whole event was Faith Pearce's idea and she also organised it. Just to top the whole day off, we then all went to Trish and Eric Hitchins' house for a barbecue in their beautiful garden. Thanks to Faith, Trish and Eric for making it such a fun day and also to Rona Joiner and Mark Harris for judging the competition, and getting the result right. This year's annual dinner was again held at Park Farm Hotel, Hethersett. Again, this is an event I find myself enjoying more each year. The photos of the meal are still up in the tower and the photo of the gentlemen of the Guild holding Faith up horizontally is a belter.

Offers from me to pose for a similar photo with the ladies of the Guild were politely turned down on medical grounds. The 2015 project has been continuing apace behind the scenes. A number of us have now been over to see the training centre at Worcester Cathedral, which we are using as inspiration for ours. If we can have a facility like that, ringing in Norfolk, not just Norwich will benefit immensely. Thanks to all the 2015 committee for their hard work over the year.

2012

There have been more peals and quarters rung on the bells this year, including a number of firsts. There have been 4 peals, a Guild peal of Stedman Caters for the Royal Wedding; Bristol Maximus by a College Youths band, including Simon Smith; Grandsire Caters and Yorkshire Maximus on dinner day. The Guild have also rung peals away from Mancroft, the most notable to my mind being the first peal of 41 Spliced Surprise Minor by a Norfolk band. Congratulations to those concerned. Following last year's AGM, it was decided that we should ring more quarters. These included first quarters on 12 for Laura Turk and Dawn Pullan, 80th birthday compliments to Andy Salisbury and David Cubitt, and Bristol Maximus by a Sunday Service band.

On an individual basis, there have been some impressive performances this year – 4 of us (myself, Richard, Faith and Ben) rang our first peal of Bristol Maximus this year at St Magnus the Martyr in London. This is something that I never thought I'd be able to do, even if I was subsequently told that my expression all the way through was a combination of confusion and terror. It just illustrates that anyone is capable of pretty much anything given the encouragement and practice. On an individual basis though, probably the most impressive achievement this year was David ringing for the Royal Wedding at Westminster Abbey, and becoming a media starlet at the same time. It's one thing to not be able to open the Ringing World without seeing David but the EDP and Look East? I thought the ringing that day was brilliant, especially with pretty much the eyes and ears of the entire world upon you so, well done David. Gilly says he's getting quite good at ironing these days, too.

Leading on from that, I would also like to congratulate the Mancroft ringers who were part of the NDA team that won this year's Ridgman Trophy 10 bell competition, the first time the NDA has ever won it.

Having seen the depth of talent that other associations have to draw from, this is a massive achievement for ringing in Norfolk. So, whilst by no means a Mancroft team, congratulations to those from Mancroft who took part.

These are exciting times for Mancroft. The 2015 project is moving forward and now the ball is rolling I think it will pick up pace pretty quickly. We're three years away from the tercentenary of the first peal, and the celebrations that will be associated with it. I think we all have a lot to look forward to.

The Twelve Bell Experience
Robert Harris

I met my wife, Caroline, at the ten bell tower of Kingston upon Thames, a nice old fashioned anti clockwise ring, full of character but challenging to ring, (unlike the modern featureless twelve that has now replaced them). After we were married, we moved down to Sussex and for the next 30 or so years we rang at the rather fine 1908 Taylor ring of eight at Withyham. So our experience of 12 bell ringing was very limited.

After I retired in 1998, we bought a cottage in the Norfolk Broads village of Horning in order to spend more time sailing. For ringing, we went to the 6 bell towers of Barton Turf and South Walsham, the 8 bell tower of Blofield, the 10 bell tower of Aylsham, but first and foremost the 12 bell tower of St Peter Mancroft.

We found St Peter Mancroft very challenging, not only the number of bells, but the weight, the draught, the springy ropes and on top of all that a rather fraught atmosphere in the tower. At least the latter is no longer the case. But we persevered and the reward for all this was the glorious sound of the Mancroft bells.

We finally moved up to Horning on a full time basis about 10 years ago and became full members of the Mancroft Guild of Ringers. And then, the experience of 12 bell competition ringing! Fundamentally, I am not very keen on competition ringing. For me, the challenge is to ring well within a team and methods which present a challenge. I quite like peal ringing, again as a personal challenge, mainly for the concentration, but I have never been drawn to the idea of one team trying to ring better than another team. However, I got drawn in to the home 12 bell team in 2006 when Mancroft agreed to host one of the 12 bell eliminators. Stedman was the method and we rang it reasonably well. We were placed third and so qualified for the final.

The finals that year were at Worcester Cathedral. Now, if you think Mancroft are a challenge, just wait until you try ringing at Worcester! Stedman again and I was to ring the 7th. We were drawn to ring towards the end of the day and the waiting around until our turn did nothing to help the nerves. We started off reasonably well, but towards the end there was a method mistake for which I was mainly responsible. We recovered OK, but were not too surprised when we finished last.

The following year, the method for the eliminators was Cambridge. We were drawn to ring at Saffron Walden, a lovely easy going 12 with a tenor of 22½cwt. I was to ring the 8th. Simon Rudd rang the tenor and I think Pike the 11th. This was one occasion when right from the word go, everything went beautifully. We were just delighted, if somewhat surprised, to find we had won ourselves a place in the finals for that year. I think that this was some of the best ringing in which I have ever been involved. The finals were to be at St Stephens, Bristol, tenor 19cwt and not too difficult to ring, but almost impossible to hear some of the bells. The method had been changed to Superlative. We managed the method all right, but could not repeat the same good ringing that we enjoyed at Saffron Walden. It is surprisingly difficult not to be affected by nerves when it comes to 12 bell competition ringing, but then you are up against the best 12 bell bands in the country.

Since those (for me) early years, we have managed to field a team every year for the 12 bell competition. Also since then, we have had the benefit of some excellent younger 12 bell ringers and I have been more than happy to take a back seat. Competition ringing is not my forte. I like to help out at practices by being a supernumery to the team to help with numbers when not everyone can be present. That way I get the benefit of some good ringing without the trauma of being in the competition ringing on the day. How's that for the best of both worlds.

Mancroft Outings in Recent Years
Richard Turk

In recent years, the Mancroft Guild has chosen to use its outings to visit London. This has also had the advantage of members being able to travel by train. The beauty of ringing outings in London is that you can walk between most of the churches relatively easily and quickly, and can use public transport if necessary. These London outings have become something of a recent tradition for Mancroft, and since the first in this series of yearly trips we have visited almost all of the towers in the City of London, and several in the greater area.

Another tradition that has grown up around these outings is the curry in Brick Lane at the end of the day. This is usually preceded by a pint or two in the Pride of Spitalfields. Mancroft ringers exploring London is not without historic precedent. In June 1894 the ringers travelled by train to London for an outing, on which they were escorted around the capital by members of the College Youths. In recent years, both the College Youths and the Cumberland Youths have been of great assistance when organising the outings.

St Martin in the Fields

2011		2012		2013	
St Giles, Cripplegate	(12)	St Botolph, Bishopsgate	(8)	St Clement Danes	(10)
St Mary-le-Bow	(12)	St Andrew, Holborn	(8)	St James, Clerkenwell	(8)
St Botolph, Aldgate	(8)	St Lawrence Jewry	(8)	St Magnus the Martyr	(12)
St Michael, Cornhill	(12)	St Katherine Cree	(6)	St James Garlickhythe	(8)
St Magnus the Martyr	(12)	St Olave, Hart Street	(8)	St Matthew, Bethnal Green	(8)
		St Michael, Cornhill	(12)		

When asked about what they most remember from the London outings, Mancroft ringers demonstrate that they don't just think about bells! The first few of these most recent outings took place in January, and a number of ringers have an abiding memory of being very cold during them. Several ringers have more fond memories of the train journeys, and have been known to admit more than a passing interest in trains in general. Many of the ringers enjoyed the fellowship and camaraderie that these outings brought to the fore: lunch and dinner usually involved a meal somewhere together.

As far as ringing memories are concerned, many of the Mancroft ringers have cited ringing at St Paul's Cathedral and Westminster Abbey as events that stand out. Our visit to St Paul's involved a quarter peal for twelve of the ringers, however all of the ringers were able to ring. One notable thing was that all the bells were rung from boxes. The visit to Westminster Abbey was part of a whole weekend's outing. The Mancroft ringers were invited to be the guest band that rang at the Abbey for New Year, and this coincided with the Lord Mayor's Procession. This experience was certainly one of the most memorable for most.

Ringing outings are usually a good social occasion and can be an excuse to try something new or unusual. The Mancroft outings have certainly lived up to this claim, and long may they continue to do so.

Westminster Abbey, 2010

Witterings from a novice member of the Guild
Chris Sawyer

I only went to Mancroft for the company and for the curry after ringing for Evensong on Sunday, reckoning that as Peter, my husband, was going to be seriously re-commencing twelve bell ringing after 18 years, if I couldn't beat him I may as well join him in the pub!

So I sat in the corner simply observing, or trying to observe how everyone found their way around all those ropes and handled bells with such a long draught, trying hard to hear the little bells; all a bit of a mystery for someone who had learned 55 years before in an 8 bell tower, had a 38 year break then only ringing on 5 and 6.

I was quite happy not ringing being somewhat overawed, not simply by the tower itself and the ringing, but also, once entering the ringing chamber, I had such a deep sense of awe and history, following in the footsteps of hundreds of ringers over the last three hundred years, it is almost palpable and still is 17 months later. I have visited many towers over the years but St Peter Mancroft is so very different and special.

Having observed for a few weeks, Simon Rudd, the Ringing Master, approached me one evening with the treble rope in his hand and said 'ring this'. 'But I have never rung on twelve before' I replied, not just that but I was terrified at the thought, 'it's about time you did then' he said and the rest, I guess, is history. I am now very happy and privileged to be a full member of the Guild, I am very proud to have been considered good enough to join.

I have also been delighted to be part of what is really more like a supportive family which extends it interests beyond ringing.

We have both forged some very good friendships with very special people and feel immensely lucky to be a part of it all.

I hope that should future ringers read this in another 300 years time, they will be able to relate to everything I and other Guild members have written. If they do then all the hard work put in by our historian, Mo Cubitt, to put all our thoughts together in book form, will have been very worthwhile.

Fund Raising Concert 2013
Anita Piper

The Mancroft ringers are a talented lot. What can they do apart from ring bells? Let me think. Well, let's say one (or even two) of us wanted to get married. We could do the whole wedding without any outside help. We have a florist to decorate the church, a priest to conduct the service, a ringing churchwarden to keep order, an organist to play, enough singers to form a choir, one or two of whom could perform a solo while the rest would make a cheerful congregation. We even have a two year old to act as an angelic page boy. After the service, 12 of the best would ring out the changes on the bells, while our in-house photographer would take excellent shots to record the happy occasion. The reception catering would be done by the cooks among us, with enough home brewed beer to satisfy the thirstiest guest.

No problem either finding a speaker to toast the bride and groom, after which our hand bell ringers would provide an entertainment. But I digress. Nobody is thinking of getting married, so this is a bit of a red herring. What we do need though, is money for our 2015 Development Fund. So we put our heads together and decided that we could put on a concert. And this is what we did in October 2013.

Our accompanist and poetry reader were friends of the ringers, but all the other performers were members of the Guild. After the concert we all had supper together and besides having a wonderful sociable evening, we made £750 for the Development Fund.

Simon Rudd and David Brown alias
Flanders and Swann

Intra-Guild Competitions
Faith Pearce

Back in the summer of 2009, four younger members of the Guild, including myself, were enjoying a bit of friendly banter in the pub following a Monday night practice as to the merits of the ASCY (College Youths) versus the SRCY (Cumberlands)! The numbers were slightly skewed, with three Cumberlands teasing one College Youth and it was suggested, in jest, that the matter be resolved by way on a striking competition between the two societies.

The idea was not taken particularly seriously until the spring of 2010, when I decided that such a competition, if taken light heartedly, might in fact be a good opportunity for the Guild to have a summer social. The idea was proposed at the Guild AGM in 2010 and received a favourable response.

Ancient Society of College Youths team 2010
Left to Right: Simon Smith, Robert Harris, David Cubitt, Eric Hitchins, Richard Carter,
Neil Thomas, David Brown, Alan Spreadbury, John Mudd

As such, I set about making arrangements, which included an 8 bell striking competition followed by a barbeque for Guild members and friends. Eric and Trish Hitchins kindly offered to host a barbeque as part of the day, the bells at Hethersett were booked and judges (Rona Joiner and Mark Harris) were secured. On the day there were three teams; being the College Youths, the Cumberlands and members unattached to either society together with past members and friends of the Guild. Each band had to ring two test pieces; a set touch of Stedman Triples and half a course of any Surprise Major method of their choosing. The winner would be the band with the least faults overall.

Teams were drawn out of a hat to determine the order of ringing, and following all test pieces being rung we all travelled to Eric and Trish's house for food, drink and the results; which were as follows:

Winner of the Stedman Triples = College Youths
Winner of the Surprise Major = Cumberlands
Overall winner = Cumberlands!

Back: Alan Spreadbury, Eric Hitchins, Mike Clements, Neil Thomas, David Brown, Peter Sawyer
Front: Ben Trent, Richard Carter, Richard Turk, David Cubitt

Back: Gill Knox, Anita Piper, Janet House, Trish Hitchins, Sheila Spreadbury, Nikki Thomas
Front: Chris Sawyer, Caroline Skinner, Faith Pearce, Jo Dorling, Maureen (Mo) Cubitt

Given the success of the day, I agreed to arrange a similar event in 2011 and Trish and Eric again agreed to host the barbeque. In 2011 we visited Saxlingham Nethergate for the competition and Barry Pickup was our judge. Three teams entered as in 2010 and the test piece was again a set touch of Stedman Triples and any Major method of the bands choice. Once again, the Cumberlands were announced the overall winners! Sadly, in 2012 the event was unable to go ahead as a suitable date where enough members could participate could not be found. However, in 2013 the event returned, with a slight twist.

As a date could not be found where enough College Youths could enter, instead we held a boys versus girls competition. The event was held at Reepham, with the test piece yet again being a set touch of Stedman Triples and any Major method of the bands choice. The test pieces were judged by Phillip Gorrod and Chrissie Pickup.

Once all the test pieces had been rung, we all congregated at Pete and Chris Sawyer's house for the traditional barbeque, ringing on Pete and Chris' mini ring and the results! **The girls won!**

Jubilee Bells
Neil Thomas (Ringing Master 1996-1997)

Having learnt to ring at Blofield in 1977 I moved to more challenging ringing eventually ringing in Norwich and joining the Mancroft Guild in 1983. For all my life I wanted to work in agriculture or horticulture, the latter was the course I choose, working my way through various forms of the industry until I ended up running my own nursery based in the heart of the Norfolk Broads.

Life had become more challenging until it reached a point in 2001 where I had decided a change was necessary, I was all set to branch off in a different direction horticulturally (pardon the pun) when a totally unexpected twist of fate threw itself into the equation.

My early ringing career had got me involved with the practical side of bell maintenance so much so that when I offered to help with the installation of the bells at East Raynham, I came away with an offer of employment at the Whitechapel Bell Foundry. I joined the firm in August 2002 and have now worked all around the UK and several countries abroad. It is however one particular project that the foundry undertook that I wish to recall. This project was to be one of the most high profile jobs for bells the country has seen.

In 2012 the country was planning on ways to celebrate the Queen's Diamond Jubilee. As in most significant historical events, bells have been cast to commemorate these occasions and this was to be no exception, Two brand new rings of bells were commissioned for towers in London, this alone was exciting enough but then an idea of genius, or madness, whichever way you wish to look at it.

The idea was floated of recreating a pageant of boats numbering many hundreds to wend its way along the River Thames, something not seen since the days of Elizabeth I, to mark this Diamond Jubilee. The flotilla was to represent boats and organizations encompassing the whole country and from all walks of life. Well what about heading the pageant with a ring of bells? It had not been seen or done before and so the idea was sown.

Plans were formulated, engineers consulted, could this be done? Many said no it couldn't, full circle bells on a moving boat would be impossible to ring. The idea gained momentum and against all the odds it began to take shape.

The next rather major obstacle was where were a complete set of bells to be found that could be hung on a boat? What better than a set already commissioned for the jubilee and so it was agreed that the bells destined for St James Garlickhythe would be loaned to the scheme. Behind the scenes a frame had been designed and was taking shape in a factory in Edenbridge, Kent. So at last it was my turn to become involved with this great scheme.

Most rings of bells are either cast new or old bells rehung in a new frame. I as a bell hanger, will remove the bells from their old frame then re-install in the new frame or simply install the new bells in the new one. Regardless I will normally only hang a set of bells once, in this case it was to be three times in three locations that I would work on them.

So in May 2012 my work began in earnest. It was decided to make sure that if all was to go smoothly, then the bells must be installed and tested in their temporary home prior to being put on the barge - so off to Edenbridge we went. The bells were delivered installed and tested and on the evening of May 17th the rather strange sound of bells ringing out from an industrial estate rather than a church was heard. The event was filmed by the BBC as it was to form part of the pageant presentation. Sadly this did not happen, but none the less we all had the opportunity of meeting and filming with the presenter, John Barrowman.

The evening was a great success, both bells and frame worked as planned. We dismantled the bells and fittings on the Friday and over the weekend the frame taken down and re-erected on the quayside at Gravesend. Take two, once again we re-assembled the bells and fittings this time in the open air, with the use of the quay crane and the fact all had been assembled before soon had it ready to go again. A test lift prior to the press arrival allowed snagging to take place on the barge, weighing in at 11.5 tonnes all went to plan.

After an amazing two weeks afloat, the bells had their first peal rung on them while passing through London. This acted as a trial for the pageant itself, although some difficulties occurred with wash from other boats and standing waves passing under bridges; but the idea had worked, it was possible to ring bells full circle on a moving boat.

The pageant went off without a hitch, well except for the weather! For the first time the public at large could see exactly how English change ringing bells worked, what a triumph for all those involved.

With sad faces we realized it was all over as the barge arrived back at Gravesend, with a chill in the wind and rain in the air we dismantled the bells for the second time.

Moving along to July and it was to be the third and final time to hang these bells, this time in a more traditional manner. The bells were delivered to the church and lined up for their blessing before being hung high up in a lofty London tower for many to hear but few to see. Independence Day, 4th July, the bells finally rang out from their permanent home.

As a postscript to this story I would like to say what a great privilege it has been to be involved in a project such as this and so to conclude it was with great pleasure that ringers past and present from St Peter Mancroft rang a peal on 3rd November on these bells to mark the fiftieth anniversary of the election of Martin Howe and Alan Spreadbury to the Ancient Society of College Youths.

The Jubilee bell frame

116

The Jubilee Bells

Norwich to York by Bus 2012
Alan and Sheila Spreadbury

Ringers have always enjoyed going on outings, visiting other church towers and ringing their bells. In 1772 the St Peter Mancroft ringers made a trip to York, being one of the centres of change ringing after London and, of course, Norwich. This was because the St Peter Mancroft bells, ten in number at the time, were in need of a major overhaul, and York Minster had recently had a ring of ten bells installed. To mark the 240th anniversary of this visit, it was proposed that their 2012 successors should also have an outing to York. It is believed that the eighteenth century ringers made the journey on foot, and it is definitely known that they rang at Lincoln Cathedral en route.

When the 2012 outing to York was first being discussed, it was suggested that ringers might travel by a variety of means. Walking, cycling, and going by boat were all suggested, but the only proposal actually adopted, by four of us over retirement age, was to use our free bus passes to make the journey. The four people involved were Maureen (Mo) and David Cubitt, and Alan and Sheila Spreadbury. We realized that this would require an overnight stop, and Lincoln was the obvious choice for that. This was firstly because the 1772 ringers had rung there and also that Thursday was the Lincoln Cathedral ringers' practice night, so we, like our predecessors, might also be able to ring there. An exchange of emails confirmed that we would be welcome to join the local ringers.

Alan studied the internet and discovered that each half of the journey could be done in four stages, so on Thursday 26th April 2012 four of us met at Norwich bus station to catch the 0955 bus to King's Lynn, this being the earliest bus on which our senior bus passes would be valid. On arriving at King's Lynn we changed on to the bus for Spalding, and from there on to Boston. At Boston we had some time to spare before the final bus of the day, the one to Lincoln, so we decided to call in at the café (used mainly by bus staff) for a cup of tea. David decided that he would like a slice of cake with his tea, but we were told by the café manager that he hadn't got any cake, only some pudding. Unfortunately, he couldn't tell us was sort of pudding it was – his wife had made it, and had neglected to inform him what it was. Our brave traveller decided to have it anyway, told the rest of us that it was very nice, but still couldn't identify it, so called it 'surprise pudding'. The final bus of the day took us safely to Lincoln where we checked in at The White Hart Hotel and enjoyed our evening meal before going to the cathedral to join with the local ringers. We were made very welcome, and after ringing we were invited to join them for refreshment in a local hostelry. During ringers' conversations, we invariably find that we have mutual friends, and this occasion was no exception. One of the local ringers, knowing that we came from Norwich, asked if we knew Becky Cubitt, as she had been at university with her. Becky is Mo and David's daughter, so an animated exchange of news followed. A very happy quartet repaired to our hotel for a good night's sleep.

The following morning, after checking out of the hotel, we boarded the bus from Lincoln to Scunthorpe. All travel plans had been perfect so far, but here there could have been a problem. Although we thought we had twenty minutes to spare, the automatic toilet was the all-singing, all-dancing type of kiosk, which goes through a five minute cleaning and disinfecting cycle after each use. Despite this we did manage, by the skin of our teeth, to catch our bus, which took us over the Humber Bridge to Hull. A quick lunch break in Hull was followed by the discovery that the next bus, which should have taken us to Leeds, had broken down. We were assured that a replacement bus was on its way from the garage, and we were relieved when it turned up, and got us to Leeds with no further problems. The final leg of our journey, from Leeds to Garforth (where we were actually going to stay) was the easiest in one way – there was a frequent local bus service, but awkward in another – we had to negotiate the Leeds evening rush hour. We arrived at our hotel and had plenty of time to get washed and changed, enjoy a leisurely evening meal and relax in the lounge. When the remaining St. Peter Mancroft ringers arrived at about ten o'clock, they were surprised that we had succeeded in making the journey safely. We just smiled as we had had an adventure!

The following day eight St. Peter Mancroft ringers joined four local ringers to ring a peal of Stedman Cinques at York Minster. The rest of the group rang at other churches in York, namely St Lawrence, St Martin-le-Grand, St Olave and St Wilfrid. We also enjoyed a demonstration of the York Minster carillon in the afternoon. Despite the inclement weather, all agreed that the weekend had been a great success.

York Minster ringing chamber

Points From Peals
Simon Smith

To the end of May 2014, a total of 403 known peals had been rung at St Peter Mancroft, making it the 82nd leading tower in the world, out of a total of 5990. A number of the historic peals have already been mentioned but there are quite a number of others amongst this total that are worthy of mention.

After the installation of the new bells in 1775, the first three peals were all rung with two people ringing the tenor. It was not until 1827 that the tenor was rung single handed to a peal when Thomas Hurry turned it in to a peal of Oxford Treble Bob Royal in 3 hours 52 minutes, which was also the fastest peal on the bells so far.

The first peal recorded which included 'visiting' ringers was on 25th February 1858 when two ringers from London, John Cox and Cornelius Andrew, took part in a peal of Stedman Caters which John Cox composed and conducted. Visiting ringers then feature regularly in peals at Mancroft. The first peal on the bells after the rehanging in 1883 was conducted by Nathaniel Pitstow from Saffron Walden and subsequent peals in the late 1880s included ringers from Redenhall, Ipswich, London and Yarmouth.

The first peal to be rung on the back eight bells was on 17th September 1889, a peal of Grandsire Triples in 3 hours 30 minutes by a local band excepting Arthur Hubbard who was brought in to conduct the peal – presumably as the local band at the time was lacking a suitably skilled conductor. The following year, Frederick Knights turned the tenor into a peal of Oxford Treble Bob Major which is recorded as the 'record weight in the method with one man on the tenor'.

Peal ringing during the 1890s increased quite dramatically but most were on eight or ten bells, including a peal of Plain Bob Major on 8th June 1893 which is recorded as being 'Trollope's first tower bell peal'. J Armiger Trollope was a member of the Mancroft band in the mid-1890s, he went on to be a noted writer on the technical aspects of ringing as well as its history and was editor of The Ringing World between 1942 and 1946, following the death of the its founder, John S Goldsmith.

Twelve bells peals were still something of a rarity at Mancroft. However, in 1894 the following peal was rung:

Durham and Newcastle Diocesan Association
6th September 1894 in 3 hours 40 minutes
5040 KENT TREBLE BOB MAXIMUS

1 Charles E Borrett*	5 Alfred F Hillier	9 Frederick J Howchin*
2 William G Crickmer~	6 Charles L Routledge	10 Francis Lees
3 Robert C Hudson	7 George Howchin*	11 William Holmes
4 Hugh D Dall	8 Edward Francis*	12 Frederick J Harrison

Composed by A.E. Durrant. Conducted by William Holmes.
The first twelve bell peal by the Association.

This peal contained seven Newcastle ringers, four from Norwich* and one from Earl Soham, Suffolk~. At the time the Durham & Newcastle Association did not have a 12 bell tower of its own, Newcastle Cathedral not being made up to 12 until 1914. Why the Newcastle ringers chose to travel all the way to Norwich for this peal when there were nearer 12 bell towers to them with ringers able to assist them such as at Sheffield and Leeds we can only speculate.

Another notable 12 bell peal occurred in 1899:
19th October 1899 in 3 hours 48 minutes
5088 KENT TREBLE BOB MAXIMUS

1 Frederick J Howchin	5 Charles Mee	9 Frederick H Knights
2 Charles E Borrett	6 George Howchin	10 Albert G Warnes
3 Frederick Knights	7 Ernest Pye	11 Frederick Day
4 William Bales	8 Edward Francis	12 William Pye

Composed by Henry Johnson. Conducted by William Pye.
First peal on twelve for the brothers Pye.

The Pye brothers (four ringers altogether), who came from Leytonstone, were the foremost ringers of their generation, with William (Bill) ringing a total of 1969 peals before his death in 1935, including many long length peals. Bill returned to Mancroft in the following October for another peal of Kent Treble Bob Maximus which was completed in 3 hours 57 minutes but later found to be false, so returned again in October 1901 for another peal of Kent which was successful in 3 hours 55 minutes and was the 50th peal in the tower.

The first peal of Surprise in the tower was rung in 1902:

13th February 1902 in 3 hours 55 minutes

5056 SUPERLATIVE SURPRISE MAJOR

1 Alfred W Brighton	5 Ernest Poppy
2 Egbert Borrett	6 Frederick Smith
3 Charles Brice	7 James Motts
4 Frederick Borrett	8 John Souter

Composed by Gabriel Lindoff. Conducted by James Motts.

This was the heaviest ring of bells on which a peal of Surprise had yet been rung anywhere in the country.

On 15th January 1903 a further 'heaviest ring' record was claimed for a peal of Stedman Triples rung on the back eight – only the second peal in the method in the tower following the first ever peal of Stedman rung in 1731!

1903 also saw the second peal of Stedman Cinques in the tower, following the long length peal in 1844, which was another peal called by Bill Pye.

In the period December 1907 to February 1908 there were three consecutive peals rung on the front eight bells, containing 7 members of the local band who were ringing their first peals including two 16 year olds and a 15 year old. The first of these peals, rung on 12th December 1907, also has a footnote stating it was the first peal by the 'newly reconstituted Guild'.

The new 'flat 6th' bell was installed in 1909 allowing for a lighter true diatonic ring of eight to be used instead of the front eight bells which had been used previously. The first peal on this new 'Gabriel Eight' was Kent Treble Bob Major rung on 11th October 1910.

Another peal of Stedman Triples on the back eight contains an interesting footnote:

8th February 1922 in 3 hours 38 minutes

5040 STEDMAN TRIPLES

1 Robert Hardy	5 George Mayers
2 Charles E Borrett	6 Frank R Copeman
3 Frederick J Howchin	7 George H Cross
4 Benjamin S Thompson	8 Frederick W Curtis
	& Douro T Potter

Composed by Arthur Heywood. Conducted by George Cross.
Rung for the wedding of Miss A May Durrant to Mr F R MacHugh on the back eight;
Potter ringing the tenor for the last forty minutes.

One would presume that Frederick Curtis was somehow unable to carry on ringing the tenor after about three hours and so handed his rope to Douro Potter for the remainder of the time. Douro would have had to have been present in the ringing chamber from the start of the peal in order to do this which would indicate that Frederick Curtis had considered that he would not be able to finish the peal on his own – something that would not be allowed today! Bill Pye returned to Mancroft again in 1928 to conduct

121

the first peal of Surprise Maximus on the bells and the first of Cambridge Maximus in the county of Norfolk (his band had rung Superlative Maximus at Great Yarmouth two days previously which was the first of Surprise Maximus in the county):

6th August 1928 in 3 hours 58 minutes

5280 CAMBRIDGE SURPRISE MAXIMUS

1 William J Nudds	5 Charles T Coles	9 George Mayers
2 George R Pye	6 Charles W Roberts	10 James F Duffield
3 Albert W Coles	7 George E Symonds	11 Edward P Duffield
4 George H Cross	8 James Bennett	12 William Pye

Composed by Charles J Sedgley. Conducted by William Pye.

First of Cambridge Maximus by 4 & 10 and of Surprise Maximus by 9.

This peal was rung almost exactly 20 years after the first ever peal of Surprise Maximus, rung at St Mary-le-Tower, Ipswich in 1908.

A peal of Kent Treble Bob Royal rung on 12th November 1929 was the first peal in the tower for Nolan Golden who went on to ring a total of 124 peals at Mancroft and who still holds the record for the most peals rung in the tower.

The 100th peal in the tower was rung on 16th May 1933 and by this time peal ringing at Mancroft had become a regular occurrence and has continued as such to this day except for the period between 1939 and 1944 when the ringing of church bells was prohibited during wartime.

Up until 1960 the methods rung to peals were mainly standard fare – Grandsire, Kent, Double Norwich and Stedman and predominantly rung on eight or ten bells, with the occasional unusual method (Erith Little Bob Royal and Winton Bob Royal both rung in 1939) and the odd peal of Surprise. The first peal of Spliced on the bells was rung in 1945 (Kent & Oxford Treble Bob Royal) and only two further peals of Surprise Maximus, both Cambridge, were rung in 1949 and 1955 and both by visiting bands. The 200th peal in the tower was achieved on 15th July 1958.

From 1960 onwards, 12 bell peals became far more commonplace at Mancroft, initially with visiting bands ringing peals of Maximus and the local band ringing Grandsire Cinques. A local band peal of Stedman Cinques was rung in 1967 (the first since 1903) with a further one in 1968. The following year a mainly local band peal of Cambridge Maximus was rung:

10th August 1968 in 3 hours 23 minutes.

5042 CAMBRIDGE SURPRISE MAXIMUS

1 H William Barrett	5 Geoffrey H Pullin	9 Brian Bladon
2 Carole A H Patey	6 Simon A B Wigg	10 Martin L Howe
3 Janet House	7 David Heighton	11 Martin Cubitt
4 Peter Adcock	8 David Cubitt	12 David E House

Composed by Roderick W Pipe. Conducted by David E House.

All were Mancroft Guild members except 6 and 9.

The first peal of Bristol Surprise Maximus at Mancroft was rung to mark the 200th anniversary of the present ring of 12:

Ancient Society of College Youths
29th June 1975 in 3 hours 39 minutes
5042 BRISTOL SURPRISE MAXIMUS

1 Trevor N J Bailey	5 Robert Dennis	9 Philip A F Chalk
2 Richard J W Tibbetts	6 Andrew W R Wilby	10 George W Pipe
3 Andrew N Stubbs	7 Alan D Flood	11 Robert C Kippin
4 Graham G Firman	8 Nigel Thomson	12 David E House

Composed by Peter Border. Conducted by David E House.

Later that year the local band rang a peal of Grandsire Cinques to commemorate the bicentenary of the first peal on the 12 bells in the tower. They used a composition of the same number of changes as the original peal, 5170, but rang it in 3 hours 15 minutes compared to 4 hours 1 minute in 1775.

The 300th peal was achieved on 23rd April 1988 by the local band ringing a peal of Grandsire Cinques.

The first peal to be rung on the 'Harbord Minor Ten', using bells 2 – 11, was rung to mark the death of Nolan Golden:

St Peter Mancroft Guild
4th November 1991 in 3 hours 22 minutes
5039 GRANDSIRE CATERS

1 David R M Heighton	6 John A Cox
2 Maureen P Cubitt	7 Andrew J Salisbury
3 Joanna K Dorling	8 J Michael Roberts
4 Thomas R Roast	9 Martin Cubitt
5 Richard P J Carter	10 David Cubitt

Composed by Albert M Tyler. Conducted by David Heighton.
In memory of Frank Nolan Golden (1908-1991),
Member of the Guild 1932-1970 and Master 1962-1968.

An additional treble bell, to allow a lighter ring of 10 to be used, was given in 1997 by Clifford Bird, a long-standing member of the St Peter Mancroft Guild, and the first peal on the 'Clifford Bird Ten' was rung later that year:

Norwich Diocesan Association
7th September 1997 in 3 hours 12 minutes
5090 STEDMAN CATERS

1 David R M Heighton	6 Frank C Price
2 Robert E J Dennis	7 Trevor N J Bailey
3 Joanna K Dorling	8 Martin Cubitt
4 Thomas R Roast	9 George W Pipe
5 David Cubitt	10 Gilbert E Larter

Composed and conducted by Robert E J Dennis.
Rung as a 90th birthday compliment to Clifford Bird, donor of the treble bell of this ring.

David Cubitt became only the second person to achieve 100 peals on the bells with a peal of Grandsire Cinques on 29th January 2011.

The first peal of Minor in the tower was rung on 30th December 2012 when a peal of Surprise Minor in 7 methods was rung on front six bells of the Clifford Bird Ten.

The 400th peal in the tower was rung by the local band the following year:

Norwich Diocesan Association

4th August 2013 in 3 hours 35 minutes

5067 STEDMAN CINQUES

1 Patricia Hitchins	5 Thomas R Roast	9 Michael G Clements
2 Janet House	6 Faith J Pearce	10 Neil M Thomas
3 David C Brown	7 Simon J T Smith	11 Richard P J Carter
4 Gillian H Knox	8 Simon A Rudd	12 Ben Trent

Composed by Mark R Eccleston. Conducted by David C Brown.
Rung as a Golden Wedding compliment to Mo and David Cubitt.
A St Peter Mancroft Guild peal.

A Vision for the Future
Simon Rudd (Ringing Master)

I can't remember when 2015 and the importance of it to the St Peter Mancroft Guild was first mentioned at one of our AGMs, but it was Steve Day who first raised the subject. How might we celebrate the anniversary of the ringing of the very first peal on 2nd May 1715?

In our tower we are proud to display the magnificent board commemorating this feat. Not only do we have this board, but making a unique 'triptych', we have those commemorating the very first peals of Grandsire and Stedman. The sense of history weighs heavily on my shoulders on every occasion I enter the ringing chamber. In modern times over 5000 peals are rung in towers and on handbells across the ringing world every year.

Back to Steve and his question. It is fair to say that, for a couple of years at least, we ignored him and concentrated on more short-term subjects and the usual minutiae that trouble and perplex small organisations. There came a time, in 2012, I think, when we began to consider the subject more seriously. There were some decisions which were quite easy to make. We should invite the National Twelve Bell Contest to hold their final in Norwich in 2015; we should have a celebratory weekend on the actual anniversary.

I began to think about the impact of that original achievement. The ringing of a peal does not now attract the interest of hundreds of listeners and is not lauded in the general press. There is not any individual ringing performance that we could possibly complete that ringers would still be talking about in 2015. I did feel however that we should try and leave some form of legacy for future generations of ringers.

What are the key aspects about St Peter Mancroft's bells and ringers? We have a heritage and ringing history like no other tower. Our bells are notoriously difficult because of the long draught of rope. Because our bells are so tough to ring, we have never taught people the art of ringing from scratch.

How might we leave behind us something that would address all three of those themes?

One of the principal reasons why our bells are so difficult is a direct result of the re-modelling of the church in the 1880s. In order to allow more light into the nave, the boarding which separated the tower from the church was removed, exposing the existing ringing gallery, half-way up the West window. Our Victorian predecessors presumably adopted the inverse of the well-known adage, in that they required the ringers to be 'heard and not seen' quite so much. The ancient ringing gallery from which all of the historic performances in the tower were performed, was therefore taken down. For an idea of how atmospheric the old chamber was, seek out the painting by Henry Ninham of the ringers in action in the nineteenth century.

This destructive act added at least 7 metres to the length of the bell-ropes, requiring three sets of rope guides and leaves us with the difficulties that we currently face in ringing our bells.

Much of the impact of the Victorian desire to allow light into the church was diminished in the 1970s, when the magnificent organ was re-sited to its current position. It would therefore be possible to restore the ancient gallery without huge visual detriment. That was therefore an idea, but a totally self-serving one. What came next was more exciting and innovative.

With a restored ringing gallery, we would create a space beneath. What could it be used for? Two key events helped us colour in this picture. First, as a Guild, we agreed to take part in the Norwich Heritage Weekends which occur in September each year. We

opened our tower to visitors for a number of short sessions over the four days of the event. For the most recent weekend, we welcomed approximately 300 people to the tower in just 8 hours of opening. This demonstrated to us that there was an appetite among the general public to find out what goes in our historic tower.

The second was the development of the Training Centre

for ringers at Worcester Cathedral. Mark Regan and his team have created an innovative teaching centre, using dumb-bells and the latest computerised technology. This centre enables the teaching of the ancient art of ringing in a modern context. So popular has this centre proved that groups visit this facility from as far as East Anglia.

With these two thoughts – that people are interested in our heritage and that teaching ringing can be done in a fun and modern style for old and young alike, it became clear what we should do. The space beneath the restored gallery could become a Heritage and Training Centre. In this centre we will have a set of 8 dumb-bells, linked to computer technology, enabling us to at last become a tower which teaches; not only our own ringers but in Norwich, Norfolk and the wider Anglia region.

In this space we can also draw together much of the valuable heritage we have, describing the history of ringing at St Peter Mancroft, making it purpose built, using video display and professional display materials to bring our story to the wider public.

This is an ambitious, expensive and complicated scheme which will take some time to see through to completion, but one which we believe addresses the key question I posed earlier. How can we, in marking our important anniversary, leave something behind us which will create a positive impact on future generations?

Looking up

Guild Members' Data (as of June 2014) collated by John Mudd

Name	Occupation	Learnt	First Peal	Method	Peals Total	Peals Cond.	Peals Mancroft
David Brown	Retired Civil Servant	1963 Langley Marish	1966 Burnham (Bucks)	Plain Bob Major	4622	2338	37
Richard Carter	Retired Head Teacher	1962/3 West Malling	1976 West Malling	Plain Bob Major	861	309	84
Michael Clements	IT Availability Manager	1968 Great Malvern	1971 Hanley Castle	Plain Bob Minor	1099	27	22
David Cubitt	Retired Solicitor	1947 Kirkthorpe	1953 Sandal Magna	Plain Bob Minor	737		100
Mo Cubitt	Retired Teacher	1960 Lincoln	1962 Norwich, Colegate	Plain Bob Minor	92		23
Steve Day	Marine Engineer	1968 Orsett	1971 Rettenden	7 Minor Methods	163	31	11
Robert Harris	Retired Company Secretary	1954 Langlebury	1962 Ashtead	Stedman Triples	286		13
Eric Hitchins	Retired Company Director	1942/3 North Bradley	1945 North Bradley	Grandsire Doubles	285	10	2
Trish Hitchins	Retired HR Manager	1957 Isleworth	1962 Isleworth	Plain Bob Royal	245	1	19
Janet House	Retired Priest	1965 Norwich, Colegate	1966 Norwich, Colegate	7 Minor Methods	635		26
Martin Howe	Retired Instructional Officer HMP	1956 Maidstone	1958 Wateringbury	3 Minor Methods	692	28	36
James Hughes	Retired Civil Servant	1972 Shilton (Warks)	1975 Stoke St Michael	Plain Bob Major	273		1
Gill Knox	Chartered Surveyor	1972 Wymondham	1977 Hethersett	Kent TB Major	278		23
John Mudd	Retired Bank Official	1945/6 Mortlake	1959 Isleworth	Kent TB Royal	70		
Faith Pearce	Tax Advisor	1994 Colsterworth	1999 Skillington	7 Doubles Methods	107	5	13
Anita Piper	Retired Solicitor	1976 Mulbarton	1990 Ditchingham	8 Minor Methods	31		
Tom Roast	Retired Chartered Surveyor	1951 Danbury	1954 Purleigh	6 Minor Methods	122		58
Simon Rudd	IT Consultant	1968 Great Bromley	1972 Ardleigh	Plain Bob Major	1325	385	27
Chris Sawyer	Retired NHS Administrator	1957 Maldon, All Saints	1961 Purleigh	Plain Bob Minor	2		
Peter Sawyer	Retired Quantity Surveyor	1969 Maldon, All Saints	1969 Maldon, All Saints	Plain Bob Minor	518	19	9
Andrew Salisbury	Retired University Lecturer	1948 Hornchurch	1949 North Ockendon	Plain Bob Minor	107	3	23
Caroline Skinner	Assistant Social Services Practitioner	1993 Charlton Kings	2004 Swansea	Rutland S Major	5		
Simon Smith	Sales Manager	1989 Bryanston	1991 Wimborne St Giles	Yorkshire S Major	670	33	11
Alan Spreadbury	Retired Computer Programmer	1957 Wood Green	1959 Darlington	7 Minor Methods	42		
Jon Spreadbury	Administrator	1984 Monken Hadley	1988 St Albans, St Michael	Cambridge S Major	47	1	7
Sheila Spreadbury	Retired Civil Servant	1960 Royston (Yorks)	1963 Felkirk	Plain Bob Minor	8		
Neil Thomas	Bell Hanger	1977 Blofield	1979 Wroxham	4 Minor Methods	323	10	31
Nikki Thomas	Bank Manager	1975 Long Stratton	1985 Long Stratton	6 Minor Methods	100		
Ben Trent	Postman	1996 Great Ryburgh	1999 Gressenhall	7 Minor Methods	102	14	9
Richard Turk	Returns Officer	2004 Norwich, St Giles	2006 Norwich, All Saints	3 Minor Methods	30		
Laura Turk	Teacher	1997 Fordingbridge	None to date				

St Peter Mancroft Ringing Chamber in the mid-nineteenth century
Henry Ninham